D0332281

Coding the Therapeutic Process
Emblems of Encounter

Companion to this volume:

Structuring the Therapeutic Process: Compromise with Chaos
The Therapist's Response to the Individual and the Group

by Murray Cox

Coding the Therapeutic Process:
Emblems of Encounter
A Manual for Counsellors and Therapists

by

Murray Cox MA DPM FRCPsych.

Jessica Kingsley *Publishers*
London

Copyright © 1978 and 1988 Murray Cox
First published 1978 by Pergamon Press Ltd
Revised edition published 1988 by
Jessica Kingsley Publishers Ltd
13 Brunswick Centre
London WC1N 1AF

British Library Cataloging in Publication Data
Cox, Murray
Coding the therapeutic process
1. Medicine. Psychotherapy. Use of interpretation of nonverbal
communication of mentally disordered patients
I. Title
616.89'14
ISBN 1-85302-029-X

Printed and bound in Great Britain by
Biddles Ltd, Guildford and King's Lynn

The cover design of an unidentified wreck comes from an old
photograph. However grave the predicament, reparative work
is evidently taking place. Those involved are coming to terms
with the chaos within themselves and the chaos which
surrounds them.

There is Compromise with Chaos and there are Emblems of
Encounter.

For those
whose
invitational edge of disclosure
sustains the affective life
of
therapeutic space

'It's a poor sort of memory that only works backwards',
the Queen remarked.
> (*Through the Looking-Glass,* Lewis Carroll)

Of any thing the image tell me, that
Hath kept with thy remembrance. . . .
> But how is it,
That this lives in thy mind? What seest thou else
In the dark backward and abysm of time?
> (*The Tempest,* I. ii. 44 - 50)

Contents

Preface to the 1988 edition

In some ways the re-issue of a book speaks for itself. *Res ipsa loquitur*. This Preface therefore says certain things which need to be said, because they cannot speak for themselves.

There has recently been an explosion of interest in semiotics, linguistics, and the outer suburbs of communication theory. So much so, that it now seems almost unthinkable that a book written in 1978, with the word 'coding' in the title, should not list 'encoding' and 'decoding' in the index. But this book uses the word 'coding' in a double sense. Firstly, it implies the clinician's notational task of encoding and decoding clinical material which emerges during the course of psychotherapy. Second, it refers to the patient's unconsciously coded mode of non-verbal expression which points to his particular perspectival world.

As a phenomenologist, the therapist finds that his attention is simultaneously pulled in two directions. He tries to take in all that a patient 'says' about himself through his 'appearance' in the world. Clothing, gait, manicure, musculature, facial expression, gesture and posture all 'speak'. And so does the smallest change in inflection, dialect*, idiolect, emphasis, syntax and speed of speaking. The

---

* 'DIALECT is . . . the particular set of linguistic features which a defined subset of the speech community shares; IDIOLECT refers, more specifically, to the linguistic 'thumbprint' of a particular person: to the features of speech that mark him off as an individual from those around him.' (Leech, G.N. and Short, M.H. (1971) *Style in Fiction: A Linguistic Introduction to English Fictional Prose* Longman, London).

The distinction between dialect and idiolect is also of interest to the therapist. It highlights his precision of finely tuned listening. He attends not only to changes in dialect – which often herald a reversion to dialect-laden buried feeling from the past – but also to idiolectic moderation. In other words, even the patient's 'linguistic thumbprint' may mature as his sense of security in discovering and becoming himself grows. On the other hand, idiolectic deterioration may be the first sign of regressive decompensation, possibly long before the content of speech suggests anxiety about death, guilt or meaninglessness.

therapist is also hoveringly attentive to the content of speech and its affective loading.

These verbal and subtle paralinguistic 'statements' enable him to discern markers which may throw the strong light of inference upon the patient's personality and his patterns of object relationships.

By linking outer world, inner world and corporate phenomena, the therapist tries to distinguish those aspects of personality structure which therapy may modify, and those which are likely to remain impervious to therapeutic endeavours. In the last ten years many formal and informal meetings have taken place as a result of ideas expressed in *Emblems of Encounter*. And I am grateful to those colleagues who by agreeing, or disagreeing, have made me think again.

There can be no doubt that effective clinical management depends, in part, upon the skills of observation, abstraction, nosological 'labelling', and establishing a working psychodynamic formulation. Taken together, these processes should serve to deepen empathy; without which therapy will fail. Nevertheless, within the broad frame of 'observation' there are more highly differentiated aspects of phenomenology – that is, of discerning the significant detail. These are equally needed, though they initially appear elementary. Yet it is upon them that clinical discretion may ultimately depend. And such discretion is not only that of overall management, it is also that which enables the therapist to judge the timing, and the optimal affective weighting of a psychodynamic intervention. Writing as a psychotherapist with forensic experience, it concerns me that in the rush to grapple with such 'advanced' topics as 'the psychopathology of serial homicide', other basic topics may be by-passed or, at best, given scant attention. Yet there is a risk to both patient and professional if it is ever felt that such phenomenological preoccupations have been outgrown. Indeed, comments on the psychopathology of homicide may be precarious and ungrounded, should fundamental, non-verbal phenomena ever be regarded as trivial. I suggest that the following themes can never be anything other than significant; though the significance may be direct or indirect: 'What can be learned about a patient's inner world by looking at his nails, his hands, his eyes, his nose*, his face, changes in the way he holds a cigarette or in his mode of gait . . . ?' And the like.

Whereas listening, *really* listening, has always been a major component of psychotherapeutic training, I wonder if there has been a relative neglect in clinical training of how to look, *really* look, at the patient. And paradoxical though it appears, I am also aware of an escalating interest in those aspects of non-verbal communication which may help the clinician to read between the lines. Maybe even between the lines on the face. How about reading between the lines on the face of the group-as-a-whole? And how could such things be annotated for clinical and research purposes? There is current interest in such topics as the evaluation of the effectiveness of psychotherapy, as well as in the assessment of psychotherapy outcome.

I hope this book makes a move in the right direction, by enhancing the vital clinical skill of noticing the idiosyncratic precision with which the patient himself 'presents'. Only then can inner world phenomena – the traditional domain of dynamic psychotherapy – speak for themselves.

There is one theoretical issue which was not made sufficiently clear in the original edition. I refer to the fact that once Unconscious material has become Conscious, it has yet to be integrated within the personality. Otherwise disclosure, *per se*, may merely lead to transient catharsis, so that no lasting change will have taken place.

The final word must be one of thanks to Jessica Kingsley, without whose energies a new edition would have remained a fantasy.

Murray Cox
London and Broadmoor, 1988

---

* ' . . . his nose was as sharp as a pen.' (*King Henry V*, II, iii, 17)
I have referred to other examples of Shakespeare's descriptive detail which enliven the clinician's capacity to notice things. (Cox (1988) *From Wimpole Street to Stratford: Shakespeare, Psychiatry and the Unconscious*, Journal of the Royal Society of Medicine (editorial) **81** 187-188).

Acknowledgements

The ideas developed in this book grew out of those elaborated in its companion volume,* so the debt of gratitude expressed at the beginning of *Compromise with Chaos* is equally relevant here, though there are certain specific additional debts to be acknowledged.

Margaret Stockbridge, from Australia, is responsible for the original conception, because her Family Structure Chart first stimulated my interest in Visual Display Systems.

I am also thankful to the Editor, *British Journal of Social Work*, for permission to republish, in its entirety, my article 'The Group Therapy Interaction Chronogram' (1973, **3**, 243-256).

Since I began to formulate Visual Display Systems of those dynamic processes which take place within individual or group psychotherapy, I have discussed various aspects with so many colleagues and been enriched by their constructive criticism and stimulating ideas, that it is impossible to list the names of those to whom I am grateful, even if I could remember them all.

These Visual Display Systems were first publicly presented in lectures given in Helsinki 1974 at the kind invitation of the Finnish Psychiatric Association.

Diana Cookson, my secretary, has kept my thoughts in order when my free-association tended to get out of hand! I am most grateful to her and to Jo Abbott (medical illustrator, The London Hospital Medical College) who transmuted my chaotic scribbles on the backs of envelopes into clear diagrams. The debt I owe Diana and Jo is now on record in black and white, as are my thanks to Ray Ruddick, Head of The Photographic Department, The London Hospital.

I am also thankful to Dr. Jack Kahn who kindly read the manuscript and made many helpful comments, and to Peggy Ducker of

---

*Structuring the Therapeutic Process: Compromise with Chaos, amended edition, Jessica Kingsley Publishers, London, 1988.

Pergamon Press Limited for her courteous advice and patience with my procrastination.

Finally, I must thank my family for a continuing therapeutic process, which cannot be coded.

London and Broadmoor, 1977

(The views presented in this book are those of the author, and do not necessarily reflect those of the Department of Health and Social Security.

Names, histories, settings and other identifying features have been changed. Several incidents described are apocryphal, though they are based upon a corpus of experience. This camouflage does not diminish the human predicament of the disclosers. The vivid impact of their disclosures remains.)

Synopsis

Representation is a compromise with chaos. . . .
The compromise prolonged becomes a convention.
(from *Seeing and Knowing,* Bernard Berenson, 1953)

This short book is a therapist's* manual of Visual Display Systems. It includes a chapter on Non-verbal Communication, which is a conspicuous aspect of even a silent patient's 'statement' about himself. Non-verbal communication may therefore be a VDS** adopted deliberately, or unconsciously, by the patient, though senses other than sight may be involved. It has the invaluable asset of demanding from the therapist the utmost precision in detailed clinical observation yet, at the same time, calls for the appraisal of nuance, ethos and the ambience of a total setting.

The VDSs used by the therapist are notational heuristic devices and are divided into two groups. The first is called 'Still Life' and refers to such fixed aspects of the patient's life as his kinship network, the actual 'bricks and mortar' of his housing conditions (sleeping facilities, sanitation, etc.) and his clinical history. The second is 'Dynamic' and deals with the capricious and ephemeral emotional disclosures made during counselling or psychotherapeutic sessions. The therapist endeavours to discern the significance of the dynamic aspects of his patient's response to both inner and outer world phenomena, by seeing them against the backcloth of the hard 'facts' of 'still life': e.g. three in a bed, a colostomy, a communal tap, an all-night disco next door, etc. However much the therapist tries to understand his patient in his totality, he will always wish he had a greater ability to observe

---

*For the sake of brevity I use the terms 'therapist', 'therapy' and 'patient' to embrace 'counsellor', 'counselling' and 'client'. This is not to imply a hierarchical pecking order, but simply because my own experience is 'clinical'. It becomes tedious in the extreme if 'therapist/counsellor' has to be stated on each occasion. [*N.B.* A 'therapist' is not necessarily medically qualified and the nurse is also 'at home' in 'clinical' work.]
**VDS(s) stands for Visual Display System(s).

1

and discern, so that his task of gradually 'introducing the patient to himself' at an acceptable depth and pace could be conducted with greater finesse.

The VDSs described are applicable to any encounter with a patient, ranging from a consultation in general practice to group psychotherapy. It is precisely because the VDSs are used as records of clinical encounters that, *ipso facto*, they encourage more assiduous observation and stimulate reflection. This, in turn, can foster an interest in the task in hand and facilitate the therapeutic process itself.

Timms (1972) draws attention to the incongruous fact that 'Recording is evidently of importance in social work but contemporary textbooks devote little or no space to the systematic discussion of the purpose, methods and use of such recording'. As far as I can see these strictures apply to many disciplines other than social work.

Coding the Therapeutic Process was written as an attempt to answer the nagging question posed by the clinical need to make cumulative sequential records of a weekly therapeutic group. Conventional notes written in long-hand must inevitably refer to individual patients in sequence or the group-as-a-whole. Neither alternative seemed satisfactory. What heuristic devices, if any, are appropriate to convey the evolving affective flow of the emotional life of a group? Can any single notational system be equally applicable to both individual and group work? This book is a modest attempt to answer these questions, though when all these *Emblems of Encounter* have been used, the therapist will, I hope, feel he has hardly begun. Fortunately patients always confront us with an existential 'nowness' and 'newness', however much this may be an outcropping of hidden psychic determinism.

Any notational scheme adopting VDSs in addition to written notes demands an adequate conceptual framework. Coding cannot precede conceptualisation.

The VDSs which follow are not presented because of any profound or far-reaching implications. I use them in clinical practice both as teaching aids and for purposes of recording. Though already in current use, the reader is strongly advised to wear the hat only if it fits. He may already have evolved a more useful method or not share my dissatisfaction with existing notational systems.

This is a companion volume to *Structuring the Therapeutic Process: Compromise with Chaos,* published simultaneously. The latter looks at the way in which the therapist/counsellor structures the therapeutic process as part of an executive professional function in the interest of the patient/client. A core concept, considered in depth, is the nature of emotional disclosure. One of the therapist's prime tasks is to structure the therapeutic process, so that the patient's emotional disclosure is facilitated at a tolerable depth and pace, appropriate for a specific setting and at a specific time. The therapist's personal construction of reality, his *weltanschauung*; the nature of therapeutic space; the essence of the therapeutic process; the way in which transference and countertransference modify perception; and the logistics of structuring the dimensions of Time, Depth and Mutuality are therefore all legitimate areas of concern. *Compromise with Chaos* deals with such theoretical and philosophical issues, in addition to discussing therapeutic skills. Therefore these topics are only discussed *en passant* in the present volume.

Coding the Therapeutic Process is of an entirely different genre. It is more in the nature of a notational handbook for the therapist, who seeks conceptual tools to facilitate the task of coding the affective and cognitive material which 'comes to light' during individual or group psychotherapy. It gives guidelines to those who try to grasp and retain the dynamic content of psychotherapeutic sessions irrespective of their counselling 'discipline', their level of professional experience and the setting in which they work. I hope some of the perspectives offered may enable those who cannot frequently participate in formally arranged teaching courses to formulate an adequate conceptual scheme of recording, notating or coding the therapeutic work in which they are engaged. For example, the medical student is taught how to make notes of conventional clinical work, such as how to describe a palpable mass in the patient's loin, and the social worker is trained to make notes of interviews and to write social enquiry reports. Nevertheless, when confronted with the need to describe dynamic intrapsychic and inter-personal processes, they discover a poverty of appropriate notational systems and conceptual tools. It is as though the composer is deprived of musical notation, so that the theme, harmony and orchestration which are so clear in his mind, are nevertheless almost impossible to 'capture' because appropriate notation does not exist. 'Notation' implies the symbolic transfer of material from one frame of reference to another, such as 'sound' to paper. Our concern here is with the transfer of emotional disclosure and affective dynamics to paper.

There is nothing absolute or exclusive about these VDSs. They are offered as tested guidelines to those seeking new ways of coding the therapeutic process. At best, they are one way of construing dynamic events. They are certainly not the only way! The Still Life VDSs are established or 'modified established', and full reference to original sources is made in the text. Some of the Dynamic VDSs break new ground. Nevertheless, they have the self-authenticating value of indicating conceptual dimensions and perceptual perspectives which have 'worked' in many different settings. They are readily understood by the most junior trainee, yet may be useful to the senior therapist with a lifetime of experience behind him. Not only are they useful for purposes of recording, but it is encouraging to note that they are also used in teaching centres, as heuristic devices for sharpening the trainee's awareness of individual or group dynamics. Furthermore, they were formulated for use in the rush of day-to-day professional work, as I was anxious to develop methods which would be used in the normal working situation, rather than in an idealised context or as presented in a perfected format suitable for submission to an examiner. None of us has time for endless reflection, and I suggest that these VDSs can facilitate rapid appraisal of dynamics and, simultaneously, afford appropriate notation for use in sequential case records.

Each VDS can be adapted and modified for the precise purposes for which the therapist requires it. For example, the Group Therapy Interaction Chronogram is used by colleagues in many settings and with different aims. The use of colour, personal symbolic notation and other idiosyncratic hieroglyphics allow flexibility in response to the 'job specification'.

This is not a theoretical book. It is a practical operational handbook for the 'apprentice' therapist who wishes to record and clarify his perception of dynamics within the therapeutic situation; which may seem to be, at best, confusing and, at worst, almost incomprehensible. I submit that the therapist is probably deluding himself if he thinks he has a readily available, universally applicable, theoretical explanatory scheme so that nothing surprises him! There are times when dynamics seem crystal-clear, but there are others when the therapist himself may feel caught up in an inchoate affective flow which has the characteristics of a turbulent ground-swell. It is in circumstances such as these that VDSs can facilitate the therapist's personal compromise with the manifest chaos of the therapeutic situation. They also equip him with a conceptual frame of reference within which dialogue with colleagues of different disciplines can be rapidly established.

Coding the Therapeutic Process therefore describes a therapist's endeavours to organise his experience as he responds to affective movement within therapeutic space. Goffman (1974), in *Frame Analysis: An Essay on the Organization of Experience,* discusses many allied themes, though not with particular reference to the organisation of therapeutic experience. It should be noted that *Coding the Therapeutic Process* is solely concerned with *bridging the gap between what the therapist perceives,* both in terms of his patient's kinship networks and current psychodynamics, *and the therapist's executive task of coding and recording* the many-faceted pleroma of therapist/ patient interaction. It is *not* concerned with the indications for the therapist's activity of structuring the therapeutic process in terms of precise tactical intervention. This was dealt with in detail in *Structuring the Therapeutic Process.*

This book has the sub-title *Emblems of Encounter,* to stress the fact that it refers to symbolic, heuristic devices using the VDS notation. These portray phenomena experienced within the context of therapeutic space; where therapist and patient encounter not only each other but also themselves, at a depth rarely possible in any other setting. These emblems of encounter are equally appropriate for therapy in any setting. They are in use where conventional counselling is undertaken (e.g. pastoral or marriage guidance counselling), but they also apply when dynamic group psychotherapy takes place in a hospital such as Broadmoor, where rapists and female patients may share therapeutic space 'without limit of time', and, when facilitated by a therapeutic climate, 'without limit of depth'.

One of the results of the 'shrinking world' has been the increased need for more effective communication between people who do not share a common language. This is shown by multi-lingual public notices, public address systems at airports, etc. Such a VDS as a traditional music notation has always been 'multi-lingual', and the new international symbols for hospitals have obvious implications for trans-cultural medical, nursing, educational and social work notes. Information about a patient may need to be 'read' by colleagues who do not speak the same language. VDSs of human interaction such as the differential disclosure profile (p. 58) can convey to a psychotherapist from another country the level of disclosure which a patient has been able to tolerate. A chronogram (p. 42) was sent to me by a colleague whose language I cannot speak, but the dynamics of whose groups I could, within limits, understand because of shared dynamic notation.

The two main groups of VDSs have already been mentioned and convey 'Still Life' and 'Dynamic' aspects respectively. The subgroups are as follows:

Still Life (Chapter 3)

    (a)   Family Structure Chart
    (b)   Household Plan
    (c)   Psychobiogram

Dynamic (Chapter 4)

    (a)   Group Therapy Interaction Chronogram
    (b)   (i)   Disclosure Profile
          (ii) Differential Disclosure Profile
    (c)   Interaction Matrix

CAVEAT: I am aware of the dangers of reductionism when terms such as 'psychopath', 'psychotic' or 'personality disorder' are used, though a book of this length does not permit elaboration. These terms are professional 'shorthand'. Our attention is upon coding, not nosology.

CHAPTER 1

Orientation

It is a fatal fault to reason whilst observing,
though so necessary beforehand and so useful afterwards.
(from *Autobiography,* Charles Darwin)

One of the aims of psychotherapy is to put the patient in touch with his feelings, and it is therefore a *sine qua non* of psychotherapeutic training that the therapist must be in touch with his. It follows that the patient's encounter with himself, which is so frequently an intrinsic part of the psychotherapeutic process, always carries the possibility that the therapist may be encountering part of himself which, in other circumstances, he might prefer to ignore. The therapist cannot withdraw from a painful area of experience where the patient needs to 'work' if it is to remain therapeutic for the patient. He cannot retreat from an emotional arena which he finds ambiguously threatening. This means that when we turn to consider VDSs, which are *Emblems of Encounter,* they will not only evoke and convey aspects of the patient's encounter with himself or those with whom he shares therapeutic space, but they will also highlight areas where the therapist encounters himself. He must never forget that as he works with emblems of encounter as a means of coding the therapeutic process, his perception of inter-personal and intra-psychic phenomena will be influenced by his emotional set and attitudes. It is for this reason that prolonged, monitored introspection is an essential part of any psychotherapy or counselling training programme.

   Although this book is capable of sustaining an independent existence, it is closely linked to its companion volume, *Structuring the Therapeutic Process: Compromise with Chaos.* When the therapist shares therapeutic space with a patient whose history includes, say, murder or rape, one of the questions which may be peripheral though

7

implicit, or central and explicit, is that posed by the predicament of the patient. 'How much is the patient vicariously carrying my murderousness?' Prospero answered this question in a singularly evocative phrase as he stood by Caliban: '. . . this thing of darkness I acknowledge mine' (*The Tempest,* **V.** i. 275). *Compromise with Chaos* discusses the complexity of the therapist's task of structuring the therapeutic process in terms of Time, Depth and Mutuality. It draws attention not only to the chaos within the patient and its effect upon latent or hidden chaos within the therapist, but also to the many-faceted dynamics of transference and countertransference which may indicate some degree of chaos in therapeutic space. This term is used to describe not only intra-psychic space (of both patient and therapist) in which there is room for manoeuvre and potential for growth, but also the inter-personal space which patient and therapist share. Therefore although therapeutic space is always bounded by a symbolic perimeter, it may also have a literal encapsulating boundary in the form of a prison wall, bars at the windows, or locks on the doors. I have discussed elsewhere (Cox, 1978) the way in which such literal custodial boundaries of therapeutic space can, in fact, intensify the quality of the relationship between patient and therapist, rather than trivialise it or imply that it is only an elaborate façade of pseudo-therapeutic space. In more senses than one, the therapist, sharing therapeutic space with patients in a secure hospital, is aware that both he and his patients 'are in this together'. The therapist has a key, the patient does not. This fact serves as a constant reminder to both patient and therapist of the unavoidable question which permeates every facet of their relationship: 'Under these circumstances, just what does psychotherapy mean? What does being genuine mean?' The strangely quizzical fact is that psychotherapy in these circumstances has a self-authenticating quality, because the constraints of reality are impossible to forget.

In this book, which is, *sui generis,* although it is a logical extrapolation from the theoretical material discussed in *Compromise with Chaos,* we discuss none of the meta-psychological or philosophical questions such as those raised in the preceding paragraph. *Coding the Therapeutic Process* is a practical manual for those, whatever their theoretical position, who are involved in the executive tasks of conducting individual or group therapy and who wish to use some appropriate style of notation both for the purpose of keeping records and for didactic reasons. I shall therefore not discuss the indications for or against individual psychotherapy, neither shall I refer to the elusive problem of judging the optimal timing and siting of different types of intervention. No reference is made to psychoanalytic or, say, Rogerian client-centred therapy in any detail. This is not because the marked distinction between such theoretical systems could ever be unimportant, but because both the psychoanalyst and the client-centred therapist will need to use some notational style for his sequential records (if he uses anything other than conventional written notes). If this is important for the individual therapist, then it is manifestly more so for the therapist involved with groups. Once again, it matters little whether the group therapist is undertaking group analytic psychotherapy or whether he conducts a supportive group counselling session for, say, widows or the parents of physically handicapped children. Whatever the setting and whatever the theoretical basis upon which the individual or group psychotherapy is undertaken, I suggest that these VDSs can help the therapist to clarify his ideas, as well as assisting him in the difficult matter of keeping notes of dynamic events.

A further advantage of using VDSs of human interaction is as a teaching medium for the trainee therapist or student counsellor. Whenever groups are observed through a one-way screen and students are asked to use one of the VDSs outlined here, there is an instant indication of selective perception and differential empathy. The discovery that three students and their supervisor each 'saw' the group dynamics in entirely different ways is always stimulating! Mary may have thought that Jim's silence was not worth recording, whereas Jean thought Jim's silence controlled the group.

There is, however, one theoretical perspective which needs to be stated, because it seems to be ubiquitous in psychotherapy and counselling, though it has many names. I refer to the concept of 'disclosure'.

[*N.B.* Disclosures made by psychotic patients have a paradoxical quality, matching their idiosyncratic perception of reality. They are just as 'real' to the psychotic discloser as mine are to me!]

LEVELS OF EMOTIONAL DISCLOSURE:
AN AXIOMATIC CONCEPT

I regard the core dynamic of psychotherapy as the therapist's facilitation of emotional disclosure by the patient. Dynamic psychotherapy may therefore be considered as a process in which a professional relationship enables the patient to do for himself what he cannot do on his own. The therapist does not do it for him, though he cannot do it without the therapist. The therapist facilitates emotional disclosure, which takes place in two phases. The first has a classical Freudian *timbre,* and refers to the movement whereby the Unconscious becomes Conscious, though I prefer the term Conscious-withheld. This is because what was Unconscious may have become Conscious to the patient and yet remain 'undisclosable', either through fear or embarrassment. In other words, previously buried material has entered the patient's conscious awareness, though he is still unable to disclose it to others. This aspect becomes particularly clear in a group context, and it is one of the main advantages of group counselling and psychotherapy. The group setting facilitates a further movement in the direction of disclosure, whereby the Conscious-withheld becomes the Conscious-disclosed. The total process may therefore be represented as follows:

UNCONSCIOUS ➔ CONSCIOUS-WITHHELD ➔ CONSCIOUS-DISCLOSED
(Cox, 1976)

The enhanced mutuality of reciprocal disclosures in a group setting will be known to anyone who has shared in the life of a dynamic group. Disclosure fosters disclosure, and so often a patient says 'Funny, I was just going to say that' when another patient has just disclosed previously withheld material. This phenomenon occurs in all groups, but it is declared in a particularly vivid manner when the members share a history of life events which include, say, murder or rape.

Compromise with Chaos discusses in detail the three levels of emotional disclosure which are as follows:

1. *Trivial.* This is trivial, social conversation such as bus-stop or bar 'chat'; e.g. 'I thought I saw frost this morning.'
2. *Neutral-personal.* This says something personal about the

patient, though it is not something which he feels strongly about. He is neither ashamed nor proud of it, and feels no inner compulsion to either withhold the information from other people or to thrust it upon them. It is difficult to give an example because it would clearly depend upon what it meant to the patient. Nevertheless, we might regard the following phrase as indicative of a second-level disclosure; e.g. 'I am breeding budgies' ('parakeets' in USA).*

3. *Emotional-personal.* This is something which the patient feels very strongly about, and is usually intimately connected with love or hate; e.g. 'I never had a childhood.' (This may have been unconscious until the moment of disclosure. See footnote p. 15)

I will not expand in detail upon the differential diagnosis of the psychopathic pseudo-disclosure and a genuine third-level disclosure, or indicate the many guidelines which suggest that the patient is on the brink of making a third-level disclosure. Such matters are fully discussed in *Compromise with Chaos.* However, it may be briefly said that the physiological concomitants of anxiety, such as changes of posture, gesture, expression, style of articulation and sometimes even a change of dialect, all indicate that the patient is saying something which is of profound personal importance to him. Part of the suffering-maturation process (Siirala, 1974) of psychotherapy training is to enable the therapist to distinguish a third-level disclosure by the patient, from what would be a third-level disclosure if he (the therapist) had said it. Thus, it is easy for the inexperienced therapist to assume that because a patient is talking about stabbing his girl-friend, he is therefore making a third-level disclosure. This *may* be true, but it may be an extrapolation from the therapist's personal experience, i.e. the trainee therapist thinks that if he (the therapist) had stabbed his girl-friend, then disclosing this to a therapist would be third-level disclosure at least! In actual fact, a third-level disclosure from a psychopath might refer to some other area of his life, where self-esteem was threatened. For example, he might have been teased at school because of some physical deformity such as protruding 'bat' ears or a

---

*This phrase would be a third-level disclosure if it was the patient's reply to the announcement that all budgies had to be destroyed because of a fatal illness spread by budgies.

speech defect. So that his fear of being laughed at, might be the core of his third-level disclosure, whereas stabbing his girl-friend might be relatively easy to disclose within a particular deviant sub-culture and so, subsequently, to a therapist.

It is of course quite possible that third-level disclosures may have a psychoanalytic flavour and refer to previously undisclosed dreams or other experience hitherto repressed. There might be hints of a dentate vagina, a frustrating/exciting breast or masked presentations of penis-envy or castration anxiety. Nevertheless, when it comes to discerning the deepest emotional disclosures, I suggest that the therapist has to be on his guard lest he presumes that because a patient is uncovering sexual material he is, *ipso facto,* making the deepest possible emotional disclosure. Again, it must be stated that whereas this *may* be true for one individual, it is not necessarily so for everyone. Sexual disclosure may, in fact, be a defence. It might serve as a delaying tactic to keep the inexperienced therapist 'happy'! There may be deeper existential fears of non-being than can be conveyed in genital, anal or even oral terms, so that even the pre-oral stage does not seem early enough.

Before we turn to consider those emblems of encounter, namely VDSs of human interaction used by the therapist, the following chapter is devoted to the patient's own VDS. I refer to those non-verbal methods of communication by which he indicates affective aspects of his inner world. The study of non-verbal communication is a *sine qua non* in all counselling and psychotherapeutic work. It is for this reason that I have included such a chapter in this book, which is otherwise devoted to various VDSs which are heuristic devices for coding the therapeutic process. It gathers together various themes which stress the importance of non-verbal communication between those who share therapeutic space, remembering that it is not only the patient who uses non-verbal communication. Many of the ideas conveyed in *Compromise with Chaos* indicate that the way in which the therapist structures the therapeutic process would be severely restricted if he had to rely entirely upon verbal methods of communication. Gesture, expression, posture, direction and fixity of gaze may all confirm or, *per contra,* contradict verbal communication. Thus even a fleeting glance may disclose an engaging smile, a furtive dismissal, an angry incursive intrusion or an apathetic 'lostness'.

I recall an interview of an hour's duration in which the patient only looked me in the eye for about thirty seconds. It was when I indicated that for fifty minutes she had been talking about her symptoms and all the things that were wrong in her family life. 'What are the good memories you look back on?' At this question the patient, whose gaze had been scanning every corner of the room like a searchlight, suddenly beamed directly at me, smiled warmly and said 'Ah, yes, . . . tennis!' Another patient found it difficult to express anger and, with him, the situation was reversed, so that direct eye contact conveyed a laser beam of destructiveness towards a particular person or episode in his history. In the former encounter direct gaze implied safety and warmth, whereas the latter implied cold antagonism.

Paralinguistic overtones are always profoundly significant and enable the speaker to 'say' more than his 'naked' words could utter on their own. Changes of rhythm; fluctuations of dialect; the exposive outburst; the staccato, truncated, lacrymose utterance; the restrained, carefully phrased, even flow of a formal speech; the barely disguised giggle; the brink of tears; the incipient yawn . . . all 'colour' the words 'spoken'.

The therapist may use VDSs for clarifying, retaining, teaching or sharing with colleagues, various aspects of verbal and non-verbal communication. The term 'clinical notes' can sound remarkably sterile and boring. I hope to indicate that the use of appropriate VDSs can transform what is traditionally regarded as a chore into an activity which becomes so interesting that it actually enhances clinical observation. The use of appropriate visual notation reduces time spent in describing dynamic aspects of the therapeutic process. The way in which the therapist structures and construes events will permeate his conception of why, when and what he records and it is for this reason that these VDSs are personal. Their flexibility also implies their universal applicability.

I have already referred to the cursory reference to such terms as 'therapeutic process'; 'therapeutic space' and 'structuring' (which may be *primary,* i.e. what the therapist *is* in therapeutic space, or *secondary,* i.e. what the therapist *does* in therapeutic space). Structuring is a professional activity focused on the prevailing needs of the patient and uses the dimensions of Time, Depth and Mutuality. These terms are considered from many different perspectives in *Compromise with Chaos* and I do not intend to elaborate upon them here, though I have already made the exception which proves the rule with reference to the concept of *levels of disclosure.* This is because I regard it as axiomatic and pervasive in all counselling and psychotherapy. It is relevant to psychoanalytic theory which stresses the significance of repressed material entering consciousness. It is implicit in conventional counselling. It links and demarcates: Group Discussion (Topic Orientated), Group Counselling (Problem Orientated) and Group Psychotherapy (Personality Orientated) (Thompson and Kahn, 1970). It is a concept readily understood by a nurse in his first week in a psychiatric ward, yet it serves as a stimulating basis for discussion at an international meeting of experienced therapists.

The cardinal feature of psychodynamic 'free-association' is that there is no depth control, i.e. all disclosure levels are acceptable, whereas in conventional counselling or therapeutic 'discussions' there may be a veto imposed upon third-level disclosure. It is *not always* appropriate to encourage such affective disclosures as 'I want to kill . . . fuck . . . love . . .'. Damage can be done if the erroneous idea prevails that a 'good' session is judged by the degree of aggression expressed! 'Ripeness is all.' Judging Time, Depth and Mutuality is of the essence of structuring the therapeutic process. Differential disclosure 'control' is a feature which distinguishes 'deep' psychotherapy (which has no disclosure controls) from more superficial counselling, though both may be almost life-saving in a particular situation, and almost death-encouraging if wrongly judged.

The concept of disclosure levels is closely linked to a VDS known as a 'disclosure profile' (p. 55). This shows at a glance how the patient is using the opportunity for 'opening up' in an individual or group session. It is therefore an exceptionally useful concept both theoretically and practically, because it gives indications of the capacity of the patient to 'use' psychotherapy as well as providing prognostic implications. Disclosure potential is linked to prognosis. It is shown in its most extreme application when patients convicted of 'the basic crimes' (murder, incest, etc.) are members of a therapeutic group 'without limit of time' and 'without limit of depth' (i.e. the patient is given no injunction to limit disclosures to a first and second level. The invitation to free-association is an invitation to third-level disclosure.)

'When I first joined the group *my words were just words*' (first-level disclosure) . . . (what are they becoming?) . . . *'They're becoming me.'* (third-level disclosures).*

A caveat must be repeated. This book is *not* concerned with how to elicit (or delay) third-level disclosures or how to deal with them when they arise. Such matters are dealt with in *Compromise with Chaos.* Here our sole concern is with *Coding the Therapeutic Process.* I am not obsessed by taking notes or making records for their own sake, but I stress this discipline because it stimulates the trainee (and the relatively inexperienced part of us all) to tighten up his perception of dynamic events. A note such as 'nothing much happened today' or 'a frightening group' may be an evasive line of least resistance by a therapist preoccupied by other-than-group events, so that he cannot remember what the silence was 'about'. The group might need an incursive thrust or, *per contra,* a benign presence. Was it frightening for everyone? Why did Mary's face look as though 'everything happened today'? Was the group-as-a-whole moving towards a deeper corporate disclosure level? Why did John retreat to a first-level disclosure when Mary dived from first to third and described how she had hated her mother ever since she said 'You don't need a bra'? Such questions as these keep the therapist awake and prevent that most deadly of all anti-therapeutic acts . . . the yawn.

We now turn to consider the VDS 'offered' by the patient to the therapist in the form of non-verbal communication. We then look at various VDSs used by the therapist to capture and retain what the individual patient, or the group-as-a-whole, fleetingly offer during the transient, capricious and constantly changing affective flow of the therapeutic process.

The deepest third-level disclosures are not accessible to introspection, except in retrospect. The patient is surprised by feelings he 'didn't know existed'. He may feel on the brink of an eruption of feeling/understanding, i.e. a cognitive-affective confrontation with self: 'I am rushing towards something in myself'. See *The Secret Sharer* by Joseph Conrad and *I never promised you a rose garden* by Joanne Greenberg (1964, Holt, Rinehart and Winston, New York). Both are packed with third-level disclosure equivalents. The latter describes a patient 'at the edge of something'. . . . 'He was frightened of the craziness he saw around him because it was an extension of something inside himself.'

CHAPTER 2

Non-verbal Communication:
The Patient's Visual Display System

His eyes were crammed with all his life.
(from *All the Days of His Dying,* Marlena Frick)

The King is angry: see, he gnaws his lip.
(*Richard III,* IV, ii, 26)

When he smiled, he didn't smile.
(Anon., 1975)

. . . my words were uttered in no ordinary manner; my forehead, cheeks, eyes, colour, tone of voice cried out, more clearly than the words I spake.
(from *The Confessions of St. Augustine*)

That look told Ivan Ilyich everything . . . that movement confirmed everything.
(from *The Death of Ivan Ilyich,* Tolstoy)

He speaketh with his feet,
He teacheth with his fingers.
(Proverbs 6: 13)

Miller (1970) writes 'Psychiatry is neurology without physical signs, a difficult branch of medicine that calls for diagnostic virtuosity of the highest order', referring to general clinical psychiatry, where there may well be an organic basis, or at least a significant organic component among many relevant aetiological factors. I submit that his comment carries even more weight in psychotherapy, where there may be no neurological physical signs, by which I mean an objective, confirmable, neurological deficit which could be elicited by an experienced neurologist. Nevertheless, within therapeutic space shared by patient and therapist, there are many fluctuating, transient, though undoubtedly observable physical 'signs' which might well have vanished by the time a formal organic examination was made, so that the neurologist's report might be 'Nothing abnormal demonstrated'. For example, during the course of group therapy a patient may describe a murderous assault upon a relative or a hitherto undeclared suicidal attempt. This may provoke in a fellow-patient obvious manifestations of anxiety, to the extent that a clinical neurological examination *at that precise moment* would have indicated exaggeratedly brisk tendon reflexes, rapid pulse, dilated pupils, sweating and other non-verbal indications of anxiety. (It would have been disastrous to group dynamics, though undoubtedly interesting, if a patellar hammer had been available during the group session!) I therefore feel justified in extending Miller's statement to embrace the therapist's heightened clinical discernment during the process of psychotherapy because if 'diagnostic virtuosity of the highest order' is not available during psychotherapy, then important clinical clues may be missed. This is not an argument for saying that only medically qualified therapists and nurses should undertake psychotherapy; far from it, but they inevitably bring a particularly important panorama of experience to the therapeutic situation. They will know that the pallor and sweating of fear are different from the pallor of anaemia, though, of course, the anaemic patient may also be afraid and anxious. They will be able to distinguish the blush of embarrassment, the hyper-suffusion of a barely controlled aggressive outburst and the plethoric concomitants of cyanosis . . . ail of which may be influenced by racial characteristics. An African, a Spaniard and an Indian all show anxiety or shame in different ways. Each nationality blushes, but what makes them blush will depend upon cultural and social factors, and the actual facial presentation varies. Each therapist brings his own professional expertise whether it is 'clinical' or that of the social worker or counsellor. Each therapist, no matter what his background, will wish he had greater experience of human beings, so that he could pick up the many non-verbal clues which are there if he has eyes to see them. Each therapist's ability is infinitely improvable! The therapist is fallibly human and will miss clinical signs. In Miller's terms, his diagnostic virtuosity of the highest order will never be high enough to link what he sees to what is being said or (and much more difficult) what is not being said or what is about to be said.

The therapist may sense that a particular patient is homosexual, though he has a record of multiple rapes, or that the glamorous female patient, with a history of several abortions, has a predominantly lesbian orientation. There are many gestures which it is difficult to describe but which can be recognised as being pointers in the direction of homosexuality, although they never always imply a homosexual orientation. There is a danger that the unitiated, who may have been taught that many homosexuals hold a newspaper in a certain way, immediately leap to the conclusion that the next man they see holding a paper in this fashion must be homosexual. This is a clinical matter, and like all clinical signs must be interpreted as part of a total constellation. One swallow does not make a summer. A patient complaining of shortness of breath does not always suffer from anaemia, and a patient with homosexual gestures is not necessarily homosexual. He might be 'acting'. The reason why homosexual gestures indicate what they do is complex, and may have to do with differential association, modelling (an appropriate term in many senses), identification and other socialising experience dating back to childhood. Male homosexual gestures are not feminine gestures, and female homosexual gestures are not masculine gestures. It frequently becomes clear to co-therapists during the course of mixed group psychotherapy that homosexual gestures may almost unconsciously invite comment, and the paradoxical situation is reached where the patient will say: 'Why haven't I been asked about homosexual feelings?' A fellow-patient in a group may ask 'Is this a question you would like to be asked?' The complex world of gesture; how a newspaper is held; how a watch is looked at; how hair is brushed aside with a hyper-rotated wrist; how a cup is held; how a cigarette is lit, allow the therapist to read between the lines and sometimes make sense of what would be otherwise inexplicable. None of these modalities of non-verbal communication are absolute and binding in any instance, but they frequently form part of a constellation or, in clinical terms, a syndrome. This means that the experienced therapist knows that he has seen certain features in common, frequently enough, for a particular avenue to be explored. There is a feeling of having 'struck oil' when a patient actually asks: 'Why haven't I been asked about homosexuality?'

The timing and texture of the therapist's interventions are influenced by many factors, and the actual verbalisation is only part, and frequently only a small part, of what the patient is conveying about himself. There are 'static' idiosyncratic statements, indicated by such factors as dress, hairstyle, tattoo, cosmetics, manicure, etc. The dynamic of his words is supplemented by gesture, posture, expression, mannerisms, as well as the timing of whole-body activity such as opening a window, gait when leaving the room, explosively opening a can of coke, and so on. If the therapist had to rely entirely upon the spoken word, his therapeutic potential would be drastically reduced, and a 'deafening silence' accompanied by other non-verbal communication would be emasculated. Whole-body and part-body language both contribute to non-verbal communication, which, in turn, contributes to the totality of communication. Such totality may be registered as silence by a tape recorder, but even the most junior and inexperienced observer would not fail to note the eager expression, the averted gaze, the silent yawn or the stifled scream. I recall an incident where a patient undoubtedly had a *grand mal* epileptic fit during a group, which by some was construed as an attention-seeking performance. Previous neuro-surgical experience was invaluable. This dramatic incident inevitably influenced what I regarded as appropriate structuring of the therapeutic process at that precise moment. A doctor does not cease to be a doctor simply because he has been trained in psychotherapy, any more than a probation officer undertaking counselling relinquishes his previous professional expertise built up over the years.

Non-verbal communication between co-therapists within shared therapeutic space, where there is inevitably non-verbal communication between all members of the group, recalls us again to 'diagnostic virtuosity of the highest order'. Each pair of co-therapists evolves its own mutually significant repertoire of gestures. Each therapist will be able to supplement what the other cannot see. No single therapist can be Janusian and literally look two ways at once, and it is part of the enriching experience of sharing group life with a co-therapist that it is possible, both literally and metaphorically, to counteract the 'blind spot' of a colleague.

Non-verbal communication is particularly well documented, with over three hundred expressive photographs, by Ruesch and Kees (1956). Hill (1974) describes how

psychiatrists of an earlier generation believed that they could predict the likely mental state of the majority of the patients they met by observations within the first few minutes of contact before verbal interchange had begun. They did this from observation of non-verbal behaviour—the appearance, bodily posture, facial expression, spontaneous movements and the initial bodily responses to forthcoming verbal interaction. . . . This has now changed, and it is rare indeed to find illustrations of non-verbal behaviour in the mentally ill in any textbook of psychiatry published in the last thirty years.

In a later passage Hill writes:

The range of non-verbal behaviours by which social interaction in man is maintained is very great. Accompanying verbal behaviour they serve the purposes of emphasis, of communicating emotional and attitudinal aspects of what is being communicated.

It is this aspect of social interaction and the place of non-verbal communication which concerns us here. Charny (1966) and Dittman, Parloff and Boomer (1965) discuss body cues and other positive configurations with reference to psychotherapy. Ruesch (1955), with splendid simplicity, writes:

There are certain things that cannot be said; they must be done. There are other things that can only be said and can never be done. . . . Therapy, therefore, has as one aim the achievement of a balanced, complementary use of both forms of language.

The structuring of the therapeutic process in terms of Time, Depth and Mutuality depends upon the total impact which the patients make upon each other and upon the therapist. It is as they share therapeutic space that transactions, introjections and projections occur, that some things are 'done' and others are 'said'; but there will be much doing alongside the saying, and there is usually a verbal frame of reference to what is done. What is said and unsaid, done and undone, influences the therapist's affective response within therapeutic space and the structuring of Time, Depth and Mutuality.

The following passage from *The Cossacks* (Tolstoy) describes non-verbal communication between Marianka and Luka. Had this occurred in a therapeutic setting the 'something apart from what was being said' would influence the therapist's response to what was being said:

Marianka, as usual, did not reply at once, and only slowly raised her eyes to the Cossack's. Luka's eyes were laughing, as though something special, something apart from what was being said, was taking place between himself and the girl.

OBSERVATION AND CLINICAL OBSERVATION

Dum tacent, clamant . . . while silent, they cry aloud! (Cicero)

Every counsellor and therapist brings to the therapeutic situation his own personal and professional experience, whatever that may be.

He will always wish for more! There is sometimes a feeling among non-medical or non-nursing colleagues that the phrase 'clinical observation' is somehow fundamentally different from 'observation' in general. No one would expect the non-clinically trained person to know the significance of bulbous finger tips or spoon-shaped nails, but any professional worker who is involved with people (i.e. every reader of this book) should notice as much as he possibly can about his patient/client. He can never notice too much, provided the intensity of his observation does not prevent him from 'receiving' the affective flow of emotional disclosure. If preoccupation with counting eyelashes blinds the therapist to his patient's tears, something is seriously amiss. Though to understand fully the significance of tears (Why this copious flow? Why the solitary drop at the angle of the eye? Why the smile of achievement or the blush of shame? Why now? Why only in a mixed group? Why turning away from the therapist or the group? Why crying 'into' the group?, etc.)—like the understanding of any phenomenon occurring in therapeutic space—needs flexibility, sensitivity and the intense observation of detail and a simultaneous appreciation of the total setting.

> He hears that name of thine,
> And sees within my eyes, the tears of two.
> (from *Sonnets from the Portuguese,* 6, E. B. Browning)

Consider Fig. 1. It is all that can be seen of an unknown fellow-traveller in a crowded rush-hour tube train. Without any medical training a long list of attributes of the 'owner' of the hand can be made. If we are told that this hand was seen at 8 a.m. and we happen to hear a discussion about 'the five children at home', various inferences can be drawn about the family. Care of fingernails and personal décor seem to come before family care. Therefore an *au pair* girl may be employed, Grandma lives at home to look after the children, or the children are not 'looked after'! It is surprising how much information about the individual can be drawn from Fig. 1.

Hands 'say' so much. 'The hand probably yields more information per square centimetre than any other part of the body' (Toy and McNicol, 1974) (Fig. 2). During a group therapy session a patient's

Fig. 1.

Fig. 2.

hands may tighten as a fellow member is on the brink of a painful disclosure, because it reinforces his awareness that one day he will have to do likewise. Many facets of the life of the patient may be gleaned from observing his hands, and the feel of his hands will say even more; the sweating palm, the cold-fish handshake, the firm almost excruciating vice-like handhold, the inability to let go, etc. But, even ignoring habitual gestures, customary posture and deliberate movement, hands make obvious statements about their 'owner' in terms of such factors as age, sex, ethnic group and occupation. Compare, for example, the different hypertrophied muscle groups in the strong muscular hands of the tailor, the professional pianist, the dentist, the carpenter and those of the casual heavy labourer. The balance between skin texture and muscular development give hints of occupation. The dentist is repeatedly washing his hands and tends to have strong, muscular hands with soft nails, whereas the tailor has equally strong hands with dry, brittle nails. The golfing enthusiast 'gives himself away' by the flattening of the 'hyper-extended terminal phalanx' of the thumb (a 'bent-back' thumb!) Stigmata such as tattooing, or the scars of wrist-slashing, give clues about previous life experience; though I found a recent clinical interview both provocative and, initially, baffling. A patient wanted his tattoos removed on his upper arm, where they could *not* be seen, but left *in situ* on his forehead, where they could be seen! The 'subject matter' of the tattoos was identical! (What was this saying? Was it that he, himself, could not see them except in a mirror?) Incidentally, any therapist who has worked within a 'deviant subculture' will recall the do-it-yourself tattooing as a visual statement of peer group solidarity, at the outset of time 'inside'. At the time of release, this is often followed by catastrophic measures to remove tattoos. Adolescent hairstyle or clothing can be changed to be in keeping (or out of keeping!) with current fashion and as a sign of group identification. However, a tattoo self-inflicted, in a moment of abandoned commitment to the group, cannot so easily be removed. More conventional tattooing, such as 'I love Jean for ever', can be difficult to explain to Mary!

Nevertheless, even the non-clinical 'statement' by the patient's nails can give valuable indications of the patient's self-image, i.e. how she sees herself and, possibly, how she likes to be seen by others. The following factors about the nails are not 'accidental'. Are they carefully filed or even obsessionally 'over-filed', casually clipped or bitten? (Presumably bitten nails are 'autogenous', though I suppose nails bitten by a partner would be a rare deviation!) Is one nail carefully manicured, but larger than the others, as required for performance on certain stringed musical instruments? Are they clean? Has nicotine staining spread from the finger tips to the nails? Are they painted? Are they equally painted? . . . or is there the tired look of nails with peeling lacquer, which reflects 'the morning after the night before' of the patient's facial expression? Are they congenital or acquired? This list could be continued almost indefinitely. When similar questions are asked about the patient's facial expression, gesture, posture, gait (e.g. the 'paralysed' man claiming compensation, whose gait reverts to 'normal' when he thinks he is unobserved), clothing, with its 'statement' of financial position, social status, whether it is 'in or out' of fashion, and the many other facets of body language, they all afford so much implicit information about his inner world. (Do socks *always* worn with one of the pair inside-out indicate that the patient, himself, feels partially inside out?) And it is possible to observe these phenomena without 'clinical' experience, though, obviously this allows the observer to perceive another dimension of significance.

All these factors may be noticed in a casual meeting at the bus stop, in the waiting room, etc. But in a sequential series of meetings, such as in clinical interviews or in the regular encounters of the psychotherapeutic session, the therapist is also able to perceive changes in these external manifestations which, frequently, reflect changes in the inner world of the patient.

What a luxury, then, to have a patient who also has a face, which conveys so much and whose expression can change so rapidly, and who talks. Or who, *per contra,* in a situation where talk is possible, refuses or is unable to do so.

The patient's body may indicate that he is on the brink of painful disclosures. When they eventually 'surface' they often relate to self-esteem:

e.g. I hardly ever remember being me. . . . The most difficult thing to share would be what I think of myself. . . . I hold out my hand and there's no-one there, not even me. . . . I want to be an on-going thing in my life. . . . I didn't know the person in the mirror.

CHAPTER 3

Still Life Visual Display Systems

(a) THE FAMILY STRUCTURE CHART

Clinical teaching is curiously ambivalent in its attitude to diagrammatic representations of the family history such as the family tree of geneogram. The student on the introductory clinical course is told to draw a family tree 'if it is relevant', with the implication that 'relevance' is restricted to such genetically conveyed diseases as haemophilia or Huntington's chorea. When discussing the family history, a well-known textbook, *Hutchison's Clinical Methods* (Bomford, Mason and Swash, 1975) states:

> Note the patient's position in the family and the ages of the children if any. Usually it is only necessary to record the state of health, the important illnesses and the cause of death of immediate relatives. If, however, there is any question of an hereditary disorder one should enquire about all known relations and *attempt to construct a family tree* showing those affected and those not affected. [Italics added]

This approach is probably representative of that adopted in most teaching hospitals. It is therefore surprising to read under the heading 'Writing out the History and Examination' the following pertinent sentence: 'Simple line drawings can often convey more information than much writing'. Under 'social and occupational history' the wise advice is given: 'Try to *visualize his life,* sharing his emotions and viewing step by step his home, family, daily habits, diet and work' (italics added). If the student has been advised to construct a family tree when it is felt to be relevant and, on the same page, is sensibly advised to try to 'visualize' his patient's life, which will certainly include his family relationships, then it appears that the enormous advantages of using a family tree are being wasted. It may be reasonably argued that the family tree is appropriate if the student is interested in genetically conveyed illness, but *when the student is concerned with personal relationships and their influence upon health, illness,*

25

'caseness' with its far-reaching ramifications, then the family tree is always important. As far as the aspiring general practitioner or psychiatrist is concerned, it is essential. But a strong case can be made for its incorporation into the routine medical discipline of note-taking for every student. This being so, the poverty of references to VDSs in the otherwise comprehensive *Notes on Eliciting and Recording Clinical Information** is surprising. This is a compact document which has concentrated so much useful information in such a limited space that the addition of a Family Structure Chart would further the purpose of the summary, by providing a concise description of what is, from any standpoint, an important aspect of a psychiatric case history.

It is encouraging to note that Cormack (1975), aware that 'family relationships are generally poorly recorded in general practice in traditional records', devised the 'Family Portrait', which is very much in keeping with the points just made about the advantages of VDSs and the employment of appropriate notation. Capildeo, Court and Rose (1976) suggest a Social Network Diagram. Macleod, French and Munro (1977) use a family tree with the symbols used in pedigree charts for recording the family history. This is with reference to the causes of death of close relatives which would indicate inherited factors. The psychodynamic significance of the patient's early family relationships is said to be 'also' an important aspect of the psychological assessment. But, once again, the central rather than the peripheral place of the family tree, even where there has never been a hint of a genetically determined organic factor, is not emphasised.

It is difficult to know why such a simple heuristic device is so persistently evaded. Whenever professional colleagues, medical students, nurses, probation officers, social workers, school counsellors and other interrelated disciplines have discussed this topic in seminars, they have returned with enthusiasm, having found that what was sometimes regarded as a professional bore, namely, chronologically recording the family history, had now become of particular interest. '. . . It conveys so much, so quickly.' 'I have suddenly found that I can remember family histories, whereas I used to get muddled.'

---

*Drawn up by the Teaching Committee of the Department of Psychiatry, Maudsley and Bethlem Royal Hospitals, OUP, 1973. [*N.B.* It suggests a life-chart in suitable cases, but not a family tree.]

Timms (1972) notes that 'recording is either taught on the job or tends to fall between the academic centre and the fieldwork placement'. I suggest that VDSs, whether 'Still Life' or 'Dynamic', can be reciprocally beneficial to both 'the academic centre and the fieldwork placement'. In my experience, colleagues working with VDSs find that academic interest is fostered because coding cannot precede conceptualisation, and fieldwork placement takes on a more stimulating, invitational quality. Thus, even the prospect of constructing a Family Structure Chart can be prophylactic against boredom!

The therapist needs as complete a grasp as possible of the social situation in which the patient lives, if he is to understand his patient's internal object relationships and so reach a dynamic formulation in terms of endopsychic patterning. The appraisal of external and internal objects applies with even more force to members of a group. In group therapy there are manifest 'external' objects, in the form of the other patients and the therapist, who are so obviously favourable 'hosts' for the patient to invest with his own internal meaning, using mechanisms such as projection and identification. If the therapist is to form an accurate dynamic formulation of the patient's internal dynamics, he will need to know about the external world in which the patient lives and to which he responds. The Family Structure Chart is a VDS which equips the therapist to comprehend his patient's external world, in order that he may more effectively enter his internal world.

Teachers of medical, nursing, social work and allied groups of students repeatedly stress the significance of accurate note-taking. Yet so few have made use of the obvious help of visual presentation, even with such a simple concept as the family tree. Medical students who frequently find it difficult to remember clinical histories are still taught to record the family history (FH) of their patient in the following way:

Patient. *John Smith. aet. 49. Presenting with recurrent chest pain.*
Not worse on exertion. Worse when anxious or alone.

FH
Father died *aet.* 50, coronary thrombosis.
Mother alive and well *aet.* 88.
Siblings:
George died *aet.* 50, coronary thrombosis.
Albert died *aet.* 50, coronary thrombosis.

Bill died *aet.* 50, coronary thrombosis.
Patient *aet.* 49, anxious *re* chest pain.
Eileen *aet.* 44, separated from her husband. Two children. Lives in New York.

For obvious reasons this particular history (Fig. 3a) would not be difficult to remember; but, using the notation employed by Stockbridge (1968) for the Family Structure Chart, the family, though mostly dead, seems to come alive. It intensifies awareness of the 'history-laden present', using Havens'* phrase. The current patient, John, not only feels isolated because his one remaining sibling lives in New York, but is also concerned about his mother, now 88. He cannot avoid the fact that his three older brothers and father all died at 50 of coronary heart disease, and he, himself, consulted the doctor with symptoms strongly reminiscent of their fatal histories, with the reminder that his fiftieth birthday is almost upon him. The heuristic device devised by Stockbridge satisfied the criteria listed by Bristol (1937):

> If I were to judge a case record on its merits I would consider its readability, that is the ease with which one could read it and grasp the essential points. I would judge it partly on its visibility, that is the ease with which a person could refer to various elements in the record and locate what he wanted. I would want it to contain a clear, concise, accurate and objective presentation of the material.

Three recent modifications enhance Stockbridge's original plan and convey even more information. The first has obvious clinical implications, and this is simply to record medical information for any members of the family, including the patient! It is also valuable to record causes of death of any family members. Not only is this a readily available source of clinical information, but it can also indicate possible areas of anxiety for the patient currently presenting. The only logistic detail which needs to be mentioned is that if the new patient is an absolutely 'unknown quantity' (by which I mean that the therapist has no idea whether he is the oldest of eight, the youngest of ten or an only child), then it is safest to start with the patient recorded in the middle of the paper, so that the family tree can 'grow' in an appropriate direction.

The second modification is that of Paloheimo (1974), who makes the gaps between the members of the family proportional to their age. For example, if parents have four boys born within a year of each other and then after a gap of four years, a daughter is born, it is highly

*See *Participant Observation* by L. L. Havens, 1976, Jason Aronson, New York.

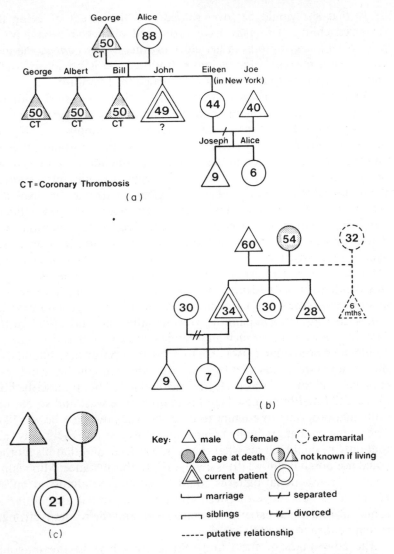

Fig. 3. Family Structure Charts: (a) John Smith (family history described conventionally in text); (b) a male patient aet. 34 (it is an interesting exercise to try to 'reconstruct' possible clinical histories or psychopathology from minimal clinical information); (c) a female 'loner' of 21, possibly an anomic recidivist.

likely that she would be 'over-valued', to the extent of being the favoured child. This may have prompted disturbed behaviour or psychosomatic symptoms in her elder brothers. *Per contra,* she may have been a mistake! Paloheimo's modification is obviously useful and it is surprising that it has not yet reached the literature.

Minuchin (1974) offers a third modification concerned with the dynamics of family structure and the transactional patterns that become established between various members of the family. '. . . repeated transactions establish patterns of how, when and to whom to relate, and these patterns underpin the system.' Minuchin has an ingenious notational system which indicates such facets of family interaction as the nature of the boundary of a sub-system. This may be clear, diffuse or rigid. Furthermore, his notation also affords the possibility of indicating affiliation, over-involvement, conflict, coalition and detouring as intrinsic parts of the transactional pattern of an established family structure. This advanced notational system has much to offer the family therapist and the psychiatrist who is able to relate at this depth with his patients, though it would be inappropriate in a medical out-patient setting or an initial interview in general practice unless the transactional patterns were actually 'shouting aloud' at the first interview. (I recall such an interview in general practice, when it would have been quite reasonable to draw the appropriate boundaries of the sub-system indicated by a mother who brought her child with earache to see me. It was perfectly reasonable for her to describe how ill her child had been, how high his temperature was, and so on, but quite inappropriate to attempt to describe what the earache was like. The young patient gradually became more restless and eventually said that only he could tell me what the pain was like, and that his mother could not possibly know! 'It is my pain!' In this instance, Minuchin's detailed transactional patterns could be completed almost at once!) He offers a new range of psychodynamic notational aids as far as family transactional patterns are concerned, and the reader is strongly recommended to read Minuchin.

The advantages of the Family Structure Chart to the on-going sequential cumulative record of hospital case-notes or those of the probation officer or general practitioner are that as new events occur in the family, so the chart can be altered. When Grandmother dies, or a baby is born, this can be added, so that the continuous modification of the chart reflects the continuous modification of the dynamic relationships. Each professional worker will have his own form of shorthand, the use of key symbols and perhaps colour.

Hamblin (1974) introduced the concept of the 'life space diagram' which he uses in school counselling.

> We can ask the pupil to imagine himself in the middle of groups of people who matter to him in his daily life and say what is important in the way they behave towards him. . . . It is useful to draw up one's own life space diagrams about a pupil based on the information available to the pupil. Sometimes there will be striking differences between these diagrams and those produced by the pupil. It can be very productive to introduce parts of these diagrams into the counselling sessions, discussing the discrepancies with the pupil. . . . Another use is to look on life space diagrams as snapshots which can reflect growth and development.

This most interesting VDS has many affinities with the Family Structure Chart, though, as Hamblin himself points out (1975, personal communication):

> The life space diagram might be used in conjunction with the Group Therapy Interaction Chronogram [see page 42]. . . In training students I stress the importance of diagrams in their case records, finding that those who develop the skill also show greater flexibility in their conceptualisation and more constructive coping strategies.

Hamblin's reflections are entirely congruous with my experience in training postgraduate students of other disciplines.

VDSs not only enable the professional worker to make more useful but also more interesting notes. Dynamic psychotherapy and the many contextual modifications that occur 'in the field' of general practice or social work are facilitated. The therapist can compare the objective 'facts' of the situation in the patient's family with the patient's presentation of the family constellation, as seen through his distorting lens of loving and/or hating. Thus the VDSs described go some way to answering the question raised by McIntyre, Day and Pearson (1972): 'Can we write better notes?'

(b) THE HOUSEHOLD PLAN

Stockbridge also describes the Household Plan. This is simply a plan of residential accommodation with special reference to beds and their customary occupants! I suspect that any reader who has worked in general practice, or in the social services involved with child-abuse, will know how important such a chart could be (see *At Risk,* NSPCC, 1976, where specific mention is made of the significance of sleeping arrangements). For example, in a small, overcrowded flat mother, father, elder daughter and the baby all try to live, sleep and watch television in one room. The only place where the parents can make love is in the same room, when the children are asleep. It is so often apparent that the battered baby was an obvious target in this confined space, where feelings rose commensurate with the baby's crying. There is no point in giving further detail here, except to say that it is not infrequent in recording a household plan to discover that a stranger, who has not even featured in the family history, suddenly appears! I can recall at least three general practitioners in a 'Balint' group saying that it was only as they completed such a chart that they became aware of an individual who, by any standards, would be a 'significant other'. This might be an *au pair* girl, a hemiplegic uncle 'who no one ever mentioned', or 'Tom, Mum's kind friend who always visited her in the evening when Dad was away!'

This particular VDS is so strikingly simple, and yet it is the obvious things which are so often overlooked.

Figure 4 is an artist's impression of another crowded flat where, say, a baby was battered.

In fact the 'household plan' the social worker or general practitioner might hastily draw would be as in Fig. 5. It will be noted from Figs. 4 and 5 that Dad is on nightwork, that there are lorry doors being banged outside, and that Sally, the daughter of six months who was battered, sleeps in the same room as her frustrated father, her brother Tom, her mother, and Brutus the dog. The Family Structure Chart and Household Plan 'speak' for themselves.

As far as a psychotherapeutic assessment is concerned, I regard these two display systems as a kind of searching sequence of special value to the general practitioner and the social worker. It is surprising how often feelings are aroused as the patient describes the lodger or the brother who has a 'better bedroom', and so on. Such demonstrations of feeling may well be relevant to current pathology and therapeutic strategy.

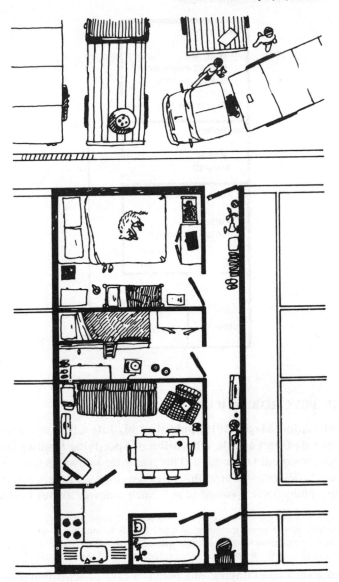

Fig. 4.

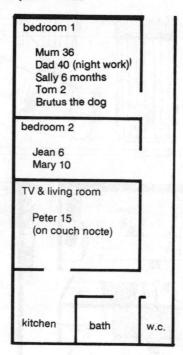

Fig. 5.

(c) THE PSYCHOBIOGRAM

In 1919 Adolf Meyer (1919) published his Life Chart, with the full title 'The Life Chart and the Obligation of Specifying Positive Data in Psychopathological Diagnosis'. This was later known as the Psychobiogram: 'a device . . . which illustrates not only our practice, but also the entire philosophy involved in it.' Such a device avoids neglecting the

examination of the psychopathological and the situational status of the patient. Well-directed attention to these settings will make the verdict safer for the patient, and ultimately also do better justice to the responsibility of the physician.

He then gives two examples, one being 'a case of schizophrenia' and the other 'a case of invalidism', and the article concludes by saying:

This brief note may illustrate the objective practical procedure of modern psychopathological studies, and how simply, controllably, and suggestively the facts can be brought into a record.

The Life Chart has been used in various psychiatric hospitals and institutes since this early pioneer work by Meyer. There are many variations on the theme, but, in essence, the idea is to have a series of parallel columns. The left-hand column contains the patient's age in chronological sequence. The chart currently employed by the Maudsley Hospital, London, then has medical data (somatic and psychiatric); duration of illness; social data; year, in parallel rows, giving a total of six vertical columns. Although there are minor changes, the basic format is on the same general lines as Meyer's psychobiogram. Such Life Charts readily demonstrate the chronological sequence of events. For example, it could be shown that every time the father was posted abroad during his military service, his wife developed an exacerbation of migraine; and every time he returned, his wife's migraine vanished, but his eldest teenage son was repeatedly investigated for loose bowel motions which only occurred when his father was home. The psychobiogram is so well documented that I will not give an example.

Strenuous mental effort is required if an attempt is made to 'link' the three prime patients, whose Family Structure Charts are given in Fig. 3, as members of an imaginary group. A therapeutic group in fact consists of eight patients, i.e. five other family trees would form the total constellation. Furthermore, each patient might justify a Household Plan and a Psychobiogram. This exercise in imagination gives a hint of the complex matrix underlying Dynamic Visual Display Systems.

CHAPTER 4

Dynamic Visual Display Systems

There is a different quality of information conveyed in dynamic VDSs compared with that in 'still life' VDSs. The latter include 'hard', objectively verifiable data. There is no doubt about the fact that the patient is aged 43, has twins aged 8, and lives in one room in an unsanitary building due for demolition. The therapist needs such hard data because it helps to furnish contextual analysis which must proceed alongside psychoanalysis if the patient is to be known as a whole person. A patient cannot be fully known if the frame of reference within which he lives is ignored. Dynamic VDSs demand much more from the therapist, in terms of his emotional response to the impact the patient (or the group) makes upon him, because they are concerned with the sharing of therapeutic space. The significance of the therapist being 'in the world of his patient but not of it' is fully discussed in *Compromise with Chaos*, and his use of dynamic VDSs depends upon his ability to be involved-yet-detached.

In some ways VDSs are the opposite of projective tests because they provide a frame of reference which can help to structure perception of what is inevitably unstructured, namely, the unfolding life of the individual or group in the therapeutic process. There is a spontaneous *in vivo* quality about the 'discovering/rediscovering' paradox of the psychotherapeutic experience. At times the therapist may have a clear formulation of current group dynamics, but at others he may be predominantly aware of a bewildering, befogging chaos. It may recall the therapist's personal experience of chaos, so that he is surprised to find there is still heat in emotional ashes long presumed dead. It is at moments such as these that the therapist is intensely aware of the process of primary and secondary structuring, i.e. what he *is* within therapeutic space and what he *does* within therapeutic space: e.g. he may foster, delay or divert disclosure. For example, a doctor whose son had been drowned in a sailing accident many years ago might be surprised to find how difficult it was to hear from a patient about a recent sailing tragedy. The ashes were not 'dead' and the doctor would be painfully aware of the demands made upon him by secondary structuring. Intense dynamic activity within the therapist may be evident as patient, benign, waiting; whereas he is aware that the very fact that he appears benign at this moment can have an incisive and a 'just-not-devastating' effect upon the patient who is about to make such a third-level disclosure as: 'It sounds awful . . . I can't really say it . . . but I almost wished he would drown . . . *almost.*'

This illustrates how difficult it is to record information about the dynamics of psychotherapy compared with the ease with which 'hard' facts can be recorded in Still Life VDSs such as the Family Structure Chart. It is the empathic quality of shared humanity which enables the patient to feel safe enough to make third-level disclosures. It would not occur if the therapist had been perceived as a cold, stainless-steel clinical specialist. However, the price that is paid for this is that the therapist himself is ever open to being invaded by the chaos which sometimes permeates therapeutic space. Structuring the therapeutic process which, incidentally, furthers the therapeutic process itself, is facilitated by perceiving dynamics in terms of the heuristic, emblematic dimensions demanded by dynamic VDSs. The experienced therapist will have more group experience to draw on than his junior colleagues, but the openness and evolving existential quality of developing group life inevitably mean that the therapist is 'at risk', however experienced he may be. He will be confronted by death, destructive violence, engulfing love, sexual deviation, masturbatory fantasies, the first sexual experience, the enjoyment of inflicting pain, the fear of authority or the desire to dominate . . . and therefore because free-association is a cardinal principle in dynamic psychotherapy, the therapist himself may be bombarded at a vulnerable point by patients' third-level disclosures. VDSs can therefore help therapists of every conceivable background and at every stage of their professional career in structuring the baffling and bewildering feelings which may be experienced during the course of group therapy. (This refers to primary structuring, i.e. what the therapist *is*—though it is closely linked to secondary structuring, i.e. what he *does*. The therapist who does not distinguish between the two will certainly come adrift when his inner world is invaded, perhaps by a chance remark from a patient.) The almost inexplicable calm which may defensively settle upon an explosive group at the point of bursting, or, *per contra,* the sudden volcanic eruption which may follow something as apparently trivial as a presumed sign of boredom (such as the rustling of a toffee wrapper, the yawn or the desultory glance at a watch by Patient A while Patient B makes his first third-level disclosure about his inability to show love), demands constant vigilance from the therapist. If this happens at the beginning of a group, then the intensity of feeling already manifest may be due to some pre-group event, and, for obvious reasons, this is more likely to occur within the context of a custodial total institution. In some ways the therapist then resembles the miller in Blunden's poem, *The Pike,* who is not aware that the prowling pike has suddenly lanced an unsuspecting chub: 'And the miller that opens the hatch stands amazed at the whirl in the water.' At this point the therapist needs to 'read' the situation in many translations simultaneously. He is aware of the 'whirl in the water'. He tries to discern whether the whirl in the group pool is a parataxic distortion of an event long ago or a transference distortion. Or whether it is a circumscribed, loculated current event.

[For example: the verbally violent and almost physically abusive over-reaction by a patient to the here-and-now fact that the therapist is wearing a new pair of shoes, might be construed as covert anger towards the therapist for failing to be 'helpful'. Whereas it transpires that the there-and-then aspect is more important when it was subsequently revealed that the female patient, Violet, was never allowed to have new shoes at home.

'Dad only gave new shoes to my brothers because they were going to be working men, whereas the girls, who sat around on their arses and did nothing, had to do with anything he could pick up in a jumble sale or steal.' The there-and-then thus explained the here-and-now, and, *en passant,* the therapist learned much about father/daughter feelings.]

The sensitive scanning attention with which the therapist views the group is fostered and intensified by the sharing of therapeutic space with a co-therapist. I have worked with many co-therapists of both sexes, from many disciplines, in a wide range of treatment settings. One of the perennially refreshing qualities of such a double harness is that whenever the therapists independently use a VDS and then 'compare notes', there is at once an astonishing demonstration of selective perception and differential empathy. A brief example was given on p. 15; a further example about silence is as follows. Therapist A may have felt that John's silence was not out of the ordinary for him, and therefore almost ignored it, whereas Therapist B felt that although John is always silent, his silence was different on this particular occasion because he smoked more and, unlike him, had not shaved. Whereas he frequently presented as being a jovial ticket-collector on the group's 'bus', he now appeared to be a silent passenger in a bus going to an unknown destination, in a foreign city, whose language he did not speak. The tape recorder could not have distinguished these two eloquent silences, although a video tape would have caught something (but not everything) which he was non-verbally saying about himself. For instance, the most sophisticated video equipment could not have registered the fact that this was the first group session for six months when John had not lavished almost anaesthetic quantities of after-shave lotion upon his beard and sat next to the girl whose favourite erotic stimulant it happened to be!

[This example describes inter-personal phenomena, but it must be stressed that Dynamic VDSs are equally suitable of the notation of changes in intra-psychic events.]

Finally, dynamic VDSs can be helpful in improving professional skills and expertise. This applies whether a therapist is just starting his training and viewing a group through a one-way screen, or whether a peer group of experienced therapists is comparing the significance of, say, paradigmatic or traditional psychoanalytic interventions with sexual murderers.

The concepts underlying the disclosure profile (p. 55) are also helpful where professional colleagues, experienced in their own field, say general practice, embark upon psychotherapy in a more formal sense than hitherto. A typical comment is as follows: 'I cannot organise the emotional content of what the patient says, so I don't know how to respond to it. This is so different from my training and experience with, say, a patient with abdominal pain. I know what I ought to do in terms of admitting the patient to hospital, giving drugs, or seeing the patient again in twelve hours, and so on.' Likewise, a probation officer may say: 'I find it difficult to organise the emotional content of what clients are saying, and therefore feel uneasy with them because I do not know how their emotional problems impinge on their management, which would not baffle me if they were not "disturbed".' These remarks could be multiplied and echo through many disciplines whose professional workers are involved with counselling, although it may not be their primary role. Dynamic VDSs, which will now be considered in detail, can provide frames of reference which facilitate an increasing sense of being at ease in a difficult, emotionally unstable field. There is a reciprocally enhancing effect between primary and secondary structuring, and the perception of prevailing dynamics facilitated by Dynamic VDSs. Each helps the other. The chronogram which follows is a relatively sophisticated and complex heuristic device, but the Interaction Matrix (p. 61) is so simple that it conveys almost 'in a flash' the relationship between current, recapitulatory and transference-distorted behaviour. This would necessitate pages of written description, the essential point of which might still elude both teacher and taught. Each VDS can be used on its own, but is of greatest value when used in conjunction with the others. This is because each heuristic device views intra-psychic and inter-personal dynamics from a slightly different perspective. Such devices are intensely subjective because psychotherapy inevitably involves the Janusian involved-yet-detached paradox of the therapist/patient relationship. Although the therapist shares in the here-and-now of therapeutic space, he simultaneously tries to retain his 'diagnostic virtuosity of the highest order', to use Miller's important words yet again. I can guarantee that if two experienced therapists, who have each had identical professional training, complete the following three VDSs with reference to a particular group (or individual) and then compare notes, it is indubitable that various new facets of the total therapeutic situation will have been perceived. Exactly what new facets become clear will depend upon their own life experience, professional training, sexual orientation, personal *weltanschauung* and many other factors which are unavoidable when man meets man within shared therapeutic space. Such an exercise is rewarding to all therapists as it helps keep them alive and prevent fossilisation, an attribute diametrically opposed to the intensely alive scanning sensitivity, which is required for optimal functioning. It is gratifying to note that these VDSs are being used by the group analyst, with his specialised expertise, as well as in an infrequent discussion group held, say, in the local authority clinic for the parents of spastic children. All VDSs are subjective, though this does not preclude their use as research tools. Reder (1978 and 1979) has made an independent study of the VDS which follows, 'An Assessment of the Group Therapy Interaction Chronogram'. He suggests that it could be developed 'as an effective research tool'. He also makes the interesting observation that the GTIC could be used to record not only the therapeutic session 'presented' in a supervisory seminar, but also as a means of recording the seminar itself. He recalls that MacLennan (1966) showed that the dynamics of the therapeutic session presented may be accurately mirrored in the dynamics of the supervisory seminar. Taylor (1961) discusses the complex problem of quantifying interactions recorded in a sociogram. Altschul (1972)[*] suggests ways of analysing interaction patterns between patients and nurses in acute psychiatric wards, and uses sociograms to present the data.

---

*Altschul, A. T. (1972) *Patient-Nurse Interaction: A Study of Interaction Patterns in Acute Psychiatric Wards.* Churchill Livingstone, London.

(a) THE GROUP THERAPY INTERACTION CHRONOGRAM (Cox, 1973a)*

[Reprinted with permission from *Br. J. Soc. Work* 1973, **3**, 243-56]

Summary

The group therapy interaction chronogram (G.T.I.C.) is a heuristic device for rapidly recording sequential group therapy sessions. It demonstrates the progressive phases within each session in addition to exhibiting dynamic patterns in successive sessions. It is of particular value where traditional methods of recording such as the tape-recorder or use of a one-way screen are contraindicated.

The introduction discusses the theoretical and practical difficulties of recording content and interaction patterns. There follows a description of the development of the G.T.I.C. from the author's individual chronogram. The indications for its use and appropriate completion notation are then suggested.

The G.T.I.C. is not the preserve of the specialist psychotherapist. It can be used by professional staff from many disciplines to record any group session whether it is formal group psychotherapy, counselling, discussion or case conference.

A hypothetical example of a completed G.T.I.C. is given below but it is emphasized that each therapist will choose his own notation depending on the dimensions he wishes to record.

Introduction

One of the perennial problems confronting the group therapist is the paucity of satisfactory methods of recording the many and varied emotional transactions occurring during a particular session. Such transactions may be verbal or non-verbal and silence, for example, may be eloquent in several ways (Seglow and Kaye, 1969). It is com-

---

*Unfortunately, at the time of writing the original article I was unaware of the paper by R. F. Hobson (1959), 'An Approach to Group Analysis'. Some of the ideas suggested in his paper, which describes 'first-order generalisations of observational records', would link closely with premises underlying the Chronogram. Helpful comments, from the UK and abroad, have been offered by colleagues of various disciplines, who have used the chronogram for a variety of purposes, in a variety of settings.

It is clear that the GTIC is a 'personal notebook' which tries to capture those elusive moments, so easily lost, which occur during the group process. Many have indicated that they have evolved their own shorthand, abbreviations and other symbols, including the use of colour, depending upon the exact ambient circumstances; such as the reasons underlying the constitution of the group, the frequency and duration of sessions, the professional expertise of the 'therapist' and the actual location, etc. The therapist may wish to note different facets of group life, depending upon whether the group takes place in prison, the local clinic or a co-educational boarding school, hospital, etc. The flexible adaptability of the GTIC allows the therapist to use it as he wishes.

The GTIC is equally useful whether The Individual-in-the-group or The Group-as-a-whole is the primary frame of reference.

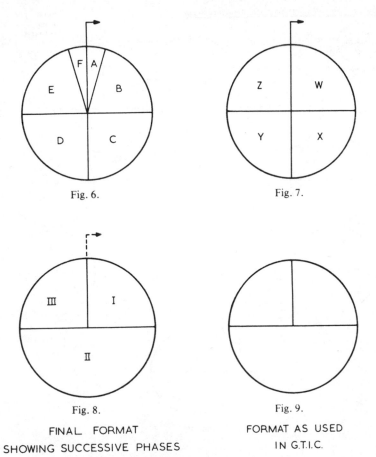

Fig. 6.

Fig. 7.

Fig. 8.

Fig. 9.

FINAL FORMAT
SHOWING SUCCESSIVE PHASES

FORMAT AS USED
IN G.T.I.C.

paratively easy to keep records of material facts such as attendance, late-coming or absence which may be expected or unannounced. However, the complexity of keeping a running record of all meaning-ful events is daunting and to take refuge in tape-recording a session merely postpones the problem and also disregards the whole world of gesture, posture and expression.

The complexity of recording the verbal content and interaction pattern of even a single dyadic interview has been known since the pioneer work of Chapple (1949) who invented the Interaction Chronograph.

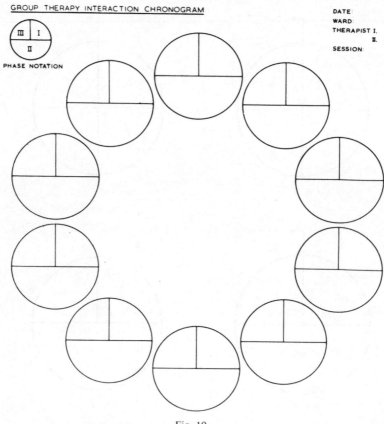

Fig. 10.

This was a 'computing machine which continuously records and integrates measurements of the time aspects of the way one person adjusts to another'. Taylor (1961) described the overwhelming complexity of Chapple's measurements when a group larger than the dyad was the object of study. Matarazzo *et al.* (1965) underline the complications of accurately observing and recording an individual interview when they write 'Under some circumstances content influences non-content, while under other interview conditions it does not'. If the relationship between content and non-content is complex when applying to an indi-

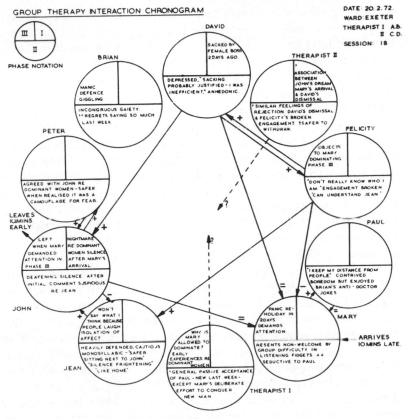

Fig. 11.

vidual interview, the relationship between these two elements in on-going group therapy is manifestly more so.

The small group may be studied by such techniques as sociometry devised by Moreno (1943) or the work of Bales (1951) which encourages accurate observation. Klein (1961) points out that it is not always so easy to differentiate Bales' categories of activity in the task-area from those in the social emotional area. The increased number of variables operative in a series of psychodynamic group therapy sessions make this type of categorization almost meaningless. For example, a patient may speak of a reality-based problem such as the conflict experienced at home when his mother does not allow his girl friend in the house. At one level he is asking for practical advice but at another level may be presenting one of the manifestations of an adolescent identity crisis. What initially appears to be a question posed in the 'task' area is an acceptable way of expressing conflict in the 'social-emotional' area.

Many different techniques have been tried in successive attempts to record group therapy sessions. Powdermaker and Frank (1953) succinctly state that 'the skill of the researcher to grasp relationships and to conceptualize them remains a crucial variable'. Schemata have been devised to minimize the problem of subjectivity. These tend to fall between the extremes of being either so complicated that a staff team consisting of therapist, critic, interactionist and verbatim reporter is necessary (Kahans, 1972), or so simple that little information is forthcoming re the group as a whole and records are confined to progressively simplified notes re individual patients (Grendon, 1972). It is interesting to note that the original critique format devised by Kahans has recently been redesigned so that most dimensions are appraised in blocks of five minutes. It is reported that junior staff find it easier to appraise sequential '5-minute blocks, and further appraisals of 5-minute blocks lead to a much easier total appraisal of 1 hour'. The author's experience is entirely congruous with that of Kahans which supports the phasic notation adopted for the G.T.I.C.

Foulkes (1964) described a Positional Chart on which 'seating positions of members are noted after each session'. There then follows a sentence which condenses the whole area of the present discussion: 'Interesting dynamic observations can be made on the basis of such a form', and it is at this exact point that difficulties arise. The question constantly confronting the therapist is to know exactly which of the plethora of possible 'interesting dynamic observations' should be recorded for therapeutic and teaching purposes.

The G.T.I.C. is a useful teaching instrument when therapists and co-therapists and other trainees share experience in a weekly group therapy training seminar. When the therapist and co-therapist have each independently completed the G.T.I.C. there is an immediate demonstration of selective perception of interpersonal transactions and a disclosure of differential empathy. Although the primary function is to help the therapist, the heightened observation and awareness of group dynamics needed for, and fostered by, completion of the G.T.I.C. could be used in research projects whether the focus is on intrapsychic or interpersonal phenomena.   Precisely because the G.T.I.C. is a type of personal group notebook for the therapist to use as he wishes, it is apparent that such a method is idiosyncratic, subjective and open to personal bias.   However, this attribute which may be seen as a defect from a research point of view has the advantage that because there is no 'correct' way of completing the G.T.I.C., it can provide a useful means of recording therapy sessions whatever theoretical viewpoint the therapist holds.   It may be used whether the group is seen as a polyfocal or unitary matrix phenomenon and any dimension the therapist considers significant may be recorded.   The precise notation adopted will be influenced by the therapist's approach, be it psychodynamic, of a predominantly psychoanalytic or interactionist perspective, or 'medical' in a more traditional sense. The latter might take the form of a record of a medical out-patients session when, for example, a group of diabetic patients is seen simultaneously by a physician.   Black (1972) runs such a supportive outpatient group which reduces the sense of isolation and of being 'abnormal' and allows the patients to experience a sense of sharing each others' limitations and triumphs in coping with the social repercussions of the disease.   In this case the G.T.I.C. could form a useful addition to the traditional hospital out-patient clinical notes.

Foulkes and Anthony (1957) discuss various foci of interest: 'We ask ourselves what went on in the group. . .'.   It has already been said that such a subjective question is open to many criticisms but so is any case record.   The reservations expressed by Bessell (1971) 'the running record can therefore only be a summary and while the aim is to make it as objective as possible, any summary invariably reflects the outlook of the summarizer'. . . though written about individual running records, apply with equal validity and even more force to records of group sessions.   However, the G.T.I.C. is a sequential record completed by the same summarizer so that, although subjective, consistency of outlook is assured.

This paper does not attempt to discuss theoretical aspects of group therapy or such practical aspects as the techniques of dealing with the

recorded material. The G.T.I.C. is solely a method of recording the
ephemeral phenomena of a group therapy session which might otherwise be lost.

Development

The author's interest in developing a simple visible record of a
group session was fired by Stockbridge (1968) who described the
Family Structure Chart. This has the 'value of transmitting a large
amount of information in brief diagrammatic form which, on inspec-
tion, may reveal significant omissions, areas of stress and even possible solutions'. It has been found that this simple format revolution-
ized the recording of family histories and not only made a complicated
family tree easy to remember but often implied potential dynamic
adaptation.

Prior to the early attempts in devising the G.T.I.C., the author
attempted to produce a method of making notes of individual psychotherapeutic sessions which gave some visual representation not only of
the content of the session but also of the temporal developmental
phases. The experienced therapist is well aware that temporal progression influences content, because statement 'n' has an entirely different emotional connotation depending on whether it occurs, say,
five minutes after the beginning or five minutes before the end of the
session. The significance of verbal and other transference phenomena
was found to be more meaningful when reviewed at a future date, if
the timing as well as the content had also been recorded. The concept
of a chronogram for an individual session evolved because the temporal sequence of events seemed devalued if recorded in the usual
way, unless 'at the last minute' or 'after thirty minutes silent resistance' was written out in longhand. Even so, such a record made for
verbosity and, if detailed, rapidly became unwieldy.

When the individual chronogram was first attempted it was on a
chart (Figure 6) which had the notation of a clockface, i.e. the session
started at 'twelve o'clock' and notes were made at the appropriate
phase of the session. *The one axiomatic fact is that the formal psychotherapy session is of a previously agreed fixed duration.* Traditionally, in individual psychotherapy, it is the '50-minute hour' but as
long as the therapist and the patient are both aware that the working

time is fixed, the chronogram applies equally to a brief 20-minute session such as might occur in a supportive but formal psychotherapy session or in, say, a medical out-patient session. In Figure 6, section A represents the initial phase and section F the terminal phase of the session. It is not the author's intention to disgress on to the wider topic of the kind of clinical notes that are appropriate in psychotherapy, the point at issue being that whatever notes the therapist would make in traditional longhand could be made on the chart, thus also recording the timing. This avoids the loss of the temporal dimension which is so important in psychotherapy and counselling, and yet is rarely recorded.

The original style of the chronogram was progressively modified in the direction of simplification and it will be seen in Figure 7 that sections W and Z represented the initial and terminal phases respectively. Finally, the definitive individual chronogram was chosen with three phases as marked in Figure 8 although the actual blank chronogram ready for completion is seen in Figure 9. This form allows maximum space for recording the crucial overture and finale, as well as providing most room for the main substance of the session. It cannot be overstressed that *each chronogram is part of a sequence and is therefore only meaningful in the light of preceding events.* A single chronogram is as meaningless as one single frame taken from the middle of a long film.

The G.T.I.C. is simply a record like Figure 9 except that the number of patients and therapists present is represented by the appropriate number of individual chronogram motifs arranged in a circle. It is then possible to record events as in the individual chronogram with the addition of the various interactive phenomena which occur in every group. Time and space do not permit a full discussion of the many dynamic processes that could be recorded and, as has already been stated, the therapist will select whatever dimensions he considers most significant. No therapist will consider every item of equal importance and his selective perception will lead him to record developments in his own way. Figure 10 illustrates the blank G.T.I.C. form which the therapist completes as soon as possible after the termination of the session.

The G.T.I.C. is also a suitable medium for recording any external factors which influence the group session such as the sudden appearance of a window cleaner's face above the frosted glass panel in a female ward or the unexpected (except by one manipulative member of the group) sounding of an alarm clock! The completed G.T.I.C. can demonstrate such factors as (a) the patient who initiates verbal exchange, (b) who tends to dominate the group by an avalanche of talk or controlling silence, (c) what the main interaction patterns seem to be and (d) the 'jostling' phenomenon which nearly always occurs towards the end of the allotted time.

The G.T.I.C. provides an indication not only of the content of the session but at which phase a particular event occurred. The statement 'there is something I must tell the group' has completely different paralinguistic overtones if it occurs in phase I, rather than in phase III. In the latter situation the patient is conveying that he feels the need to speak, *cacoithes dicendi,* but remains 'on the brink of saying many things'. This is not a recently discovered phenomenon: Dido suddenly left Aeneas who was 'full of hesitation in his fear and preparing to say so much' (Vergil). This characteristically occurs towards the end of a psychotherapeutic session and can be recorded in phase III. The content eludes or frightens the patient but the declaration of his state of 'brinkness' may facilitate subsequent verbalization, so that he can accept what he previously found unacceptable. In this way his own self-definition is redefined (Cox, 1973b).

A patient who consistently arrives late tends to feel that he is justified in having the 'last word' because he was not present to have the 'first word'. Temporal progression in a group is rarely felt to be steady, as some phases seem to drag and some go too fast. At one stage it was suggested that the author might have a special clock for timing therapeutic sessions which could be pre-set to accelerate or decelerate during the last phase! Such evanescent transference phenomena as indicated by a patient who said that the author was present at the beginning and end of the session but 'seemed to go away during the middle' could readily be noted on the G.T.I.C.

Indications

The indications for using the G.T.I.C. are so varied that the therapists' theoretical background and clinical focus will differ widely, ranging from a psychoanalytic preoccupation with unconscious motivation, free-association, transference phenomena and dream life, to, say, a paediatrician's concern to record sequential case conferences.

The G.T.I.C. is particularly useful when the established methods of recording are contraindicated. There are limitations on the advisability of using a tape-recorder during a session. Although it is an established technique applicable in certain situations, such an instrument may adversely influence the spontaneity of many group participants, especially those in total institutions. Any latent or manifest paranoid elements are likely to become more pronounced and it is not unknown for a paranoid schizophrenic to attack the tape-recorder or use it as a weapon to attack someone else. There are other contraindications to the use of a one-way screen.

The G.T.I.C. provides a useful and easily accessible method of comparing the dynamics of two sessions which may be six months apart. Thus it could be seen at a glance that a patient who always used to sit silent until the last five minutes of the session had recently been able to answer questions at an earlier stage and had even 'opened' the session. The significance of this change of behaviour will obviously depend on the diagnostic formulation, the defence mechanisms currently operating and the group matrix. The G.T.I.C. helps the therapist to furnish a current appraisal of the group-as-a-whole or the individual patient.

Another practical value of the G.T.I.C. is that if one co-therapist is absent it allows his colleague to convey information re the missed session in an established convention which is meaningful to them both, provided they have evolved their own mutually intelligible notation and abbreviations. What is applicable in one situation may not necessarily apply elsewhere. Thus a private group of neurotics with marital problems may suggest different notational demands from a group of aggressive psychopaths within a total institution with the attendant problems of security and the risks of acting-out. Edelson (1970) states that 'differentiation of socio-therapy and psychotherapy does not imply that either is self-sufficient in the treatment enterprise', and proceeds to elaborate on the complex interdependence of both elements within the total therapeutic community. The G.T.I.C. provides the flexibility which is necessary if a therapist is working with groups in several different settings.

The G.T.I.C. may be used whenever there is a need to make records of serial group sessions and is a helpful teaching aid. It may be used by therapists who have had full analytic training, by general psychiatrists, other medical and nursing staff, clergy, psychologists, marriage guidance counsellors, social workers, probation officers and prison officers. Each of these different specialized disciplines will see different uses for the G.T.I.C. It is therefore clear that each professional group will tend to adopt its own style of notation which will be relevant and pertinent to the work in hand.

Notation

There is no standard form of notation which should be universally applied, as this would be restrictive and reduce the interdisciplinary scope.

Immediately after concluding a group therapy session the therapist walks away with a plethora of remembered events and feelings competing for attention. Nevertheless, there are usually certain psychodynamic events which, seen in the light of the previous group experience, merit priority of recording. This is often at the expense of what might at first sight seems to be 'significant'. This is perhaps best illustrated by considering a hypothetical completed G.T.I.C. as in Figure 11. It will be seen that this is the eighteenth session and therefore the therapists would already have experience of working with this particular group for seventeen previous sessions. Therefore what is recorded on 20.2.72 will have been selected against the background of the earlier group experiences. The material recorded may be justified on the grounds that some new development has occurred, be it a change in an established intra-psychic defence mechanism previously regularly used by a particular patient or some relevant current social situation such as David's reaction to his dismissal from work.

Because the G.T.I.C. may be used by workers with widely differing notational demands, such as a Kleinian group analyst or a health visitor running group discussions for lonely geriatric patients, the author has used the *via media* of psychosocial terminology for the hypothetical group in Figure 11. In fact the analyst might adopt a psychoanalytic nomenclature, e.g. 'splitting and projective identification' whereas the health visitor might give quotations, e.g. 'said she thought cat was dying'. However, whatever vocabulary is used the G.T.I.C. allows temporal sequence to be recorded without actually referring to it, which is otherwise necessary in a longhand, verbatim report. In Figure 11, Jean illustrates the psychosocial quality of the recording and the arrows from Felicity marked with a + sign indicate warmth, agreement and support such as Felicity feels towards Jean and Jean feels towards John. It should be noted that John is suspicious of Jean and this is recorded with a — sign.

For the sake of clarity a few guidelines for (A) completion and (B) reading the G.T.I.C. are now given.

A. Completion

1. Try to complete the G.T.I.C. as soon as possible* after the session but do not take more than about twenty minutes to do so. The feeling responses of the therapist are important and they become reduced if too many other events intervene between termination of the session and completion of the G.T.I.C. If there are two therapists the G.T.I.C. should be completed independently if teaching potential is to be maximized. The G.T.I.C. allows for eight patients and two therapists but can be adapted as required. Absent patients, and the reason for the absence if known, can be recorded and the alteration in an established seating pattern caused by such absence is immediately visible.

2. Record absentees and any extra-group physical movements first, such as Mary's arrival ten minutes late and John's departure ten minutes early. A frequent type of acting-out, though not indicated in Figure 11, is the patient who walks out of the room in an outburst of anger only to return later during the session. It is helpful to record this type of physical movement before the more structured details of the chronogram are completed.

3. Using the phase notation already suggested the G.T.I.C. is best completed in this order: phase I, phase III, phase II. It is easy to remember who actually initiated the verbal exchange and it will be seen that John spoke of his nightmare in phase I, though this was

---

*After a ten minute 'breather' and a cup of coffee!

made easier to describe following David's feelings about his female boss which 'opened' the session. It was towards the end of phase I that therapist II made the comments recorded. It is also easy to remember how the session ended and it is for this reason that the therapists are advised to complete the three phases of the G.T.I.C. before building up the interaction lattice. Nevertheless, it is sometimes felt that the latter is of such significance that this precedes the completion of phase II.

4. Although all verbal interactions have direction, frequency, intensity and content it has been found that the recording style suggested in Figure 11 has working value. The symbols + and $\ddagger$ and — and = are taken to imply degrees of positive and negative feeling respectively, which may or may not be verbalized. It is this form of notation which is used in constructing the interaction lattice.

5. Figure 11 shows that the therapists' interventions are indicated with question marks and this is purely for notational purposes. Such therapeutic interventions may, of course, be statements but the inflection of voice may imply a response from the group. It should be noted that interventions directed to the group-as-a-whole and not to any particular member are shown by arrows which are radial but do not reach the centre of the circle. This follows the notational style suggested by Kahans (1972) for universal group phenomena such as laughter or questions directed to the whole group.

6. Do not try to record too much. The G.T.I.C. is for recording the dominant events (which might be the silence of a previously hypomanic patient) so that, at a later date, a quick glance would recall the main dynamics of the group. Thus rapid perusal of Figure 11 recalls the group held in Exeter Ward on 20.2.72.

B. Reading   The technique of 'reading' a G.T.I.C. is facilitated if it is undertaken in a systematic way similar to the standard method of studying an electrocardiogram. It is suggested that the reading sequence follows the same pattern as the completion sequence just described, i.e. extra-group events, phase I, phase III and finally the interaction lattice and phase II. In this way a rapid appraisal is gained within a minute or two.

Completion of the G.T.I.C. sounds complicated and fraught with difficulty. However, in practice, it has proved useful and easy to complete once the therapist has decided on the particular notation he wishes to employ.

(The references for the original article have been included in the references at the end of the book.) [Blank G.T.I.C. forms are supplied by Jessica Kingsley Publishers, 13 Brunswick Centre, London WC1N 1AF.]

Both the G.T.I.C. and the following VDS emphasise the importance of the maxim: If the patient does not know when the end is, he cannot know when 'just before the end' is. The reasons for disclosures occurring *just before the end* are too complex to discuss here, but, as far as recording the session is concerned, *just before the end* is likely to be 'action packed' with verbal disclosure or rapidly intensifying silence.

(b) (i) THE DISCLOSURE PROFILE

> To start with I thought group therapy was rubbish,
> but *once you start going deep it keeps going deeper still.*
> (Anon., 1976)

> We seemed to sink through layer after layer of what was
> superficial, till gradually both reached the central fire.
> It was an experience unlike any other that I have known.
> (from *Autobiograhy,* Bertrand Russell)

The Disclosure Profile and the Differential Disclosure Profile have been briefly mentioned in previous publications (Cox, 1974; Macphail and Cox, 1975), though it is only here that these heuristic devices are developed. The Disclosure Profile is a VDS of 'levels of disclosure', already referred to in Chapter 1, though the concept is fully explained in *Compromise with Chaos.*

It will be recalled that the three levels of disclosure are as follows: (1) Trivial: 'I thought I saw frost this morning.' (2) Neutral-personal: 'I am breeding budgies.' (3) Emotional-personal: 'I never had a childhood.'

The levels of disclosure are indicated by the vertical axis in Fig. 12. The horizontal axis is that of time, which may relate to a single thera-peutic session as though it were 'a close-up' of fluctuating levels of disclosure during a single session, or it may indicate the profile of dis-closure patterns over a prolonged period. In actual practice, parallel horizontal lines, as in Fig. 13, are all that is necessary because the therapist will inevitably know whether the horizontal 'time' axis refers to one session or, say, an overall pattern of disclosure for the six months' duration of a particular group.

The three separate disclosure profiles, X, Y and Z, each convey different patterns of disclosure. X is characteristic of the hysteric who tends to say too much, too soon and then rapidly regrets 'letting the cat out of the bag' and frequently seeks reasons to justify leaving the group, remains silent or never goes below a first-level disclosure, at

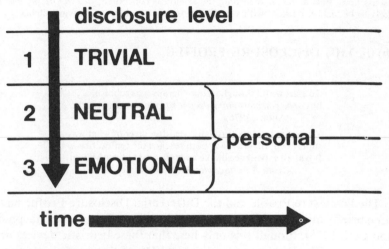

disclosure level

1	TRIVIAL
2	NEUTRAL
3	EMOTIONAL

personal

time

disclosure profile

1. 'I thought I saw frost this morning.'
2. 'I am breeding budgies.'
3. 'I never had a childhood.'

Fig. 12.

least for a long time. He is usually anxious, and his importunity, paradoxically so closely allied to the need to be the centre of attention, drives him to say 'more than was intended'. The pseudo-disclosure of the psychopath can present a problem of differential diagnosis, though the physiological concomitants of anxiety and the therapist's awareness of the circumstances usually enable him to distinguish the two. The patient who may be described as a hysterical psychopath perhaps presents the greatest difficulty. But, as he will be the first to admit, in a group situation where there are eight similar patients who all know that 'the most difficult person to con is another con', he finds that it is almost impossible to convince such a group that a pseudo-disclosure is in fact genuine. One of the most rewarding moments in the whole of psychotherapy is when a psychopath, whose life-history so often seems to show a progressive hardening and dis- tancing in all relationships because of repeated betrayal, and the experience of being let down by people he trusted, 'dips' sharply down into the realm of *genuine* third-level disclosure. When he starts in a group he will not trust the other members or the therapist (why should he?). He finds safety in first-level disclosures. When he does begin to talk it will usually be in terms of criticising the staff, other and earlier authority figures, then his peers, and last, if ever, himself. His early 'deep' disclosures in the group are usually pseudo-disclosures. But when the psychopath eventually makes a third-level disclosure, it is as unmistakable as a double-decker bus. (The important underlying question is the relationship between a genuine third-level disclosure and prognosis.)

Figure 13 X is characteristic of the premature disclosure of a hysteric or the pseudo-disclosure of a psychopath. Figure 13 Y indicates mini- mal personal disclosure, which might be explicable in terms of anxiety

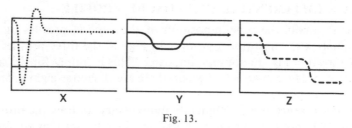

| X | Y | Z |

Fig. 13.

or wisdom! This particular profile is common at the beginning of group sessions with psychopaths and personality disorders, who wait for a group consensus which could be summarised as follows. 'I will talk if you will.' As each patient feels the same, little movement is likely to occur till genuine feeling is ventilated, either in terms of anger towards the therapist or other here-and-now reality-based affective thrust. There is then a chain reaction, so that once Tom has reached a second or third-level disclosure, he will be rapidly followed by Bob, and maybe Mary and Jean. The intensely introverted neurotic or schizoid personality may take a very long time to get beyond profile Y.

Figure 13 Z indicates a progressive movement towards third-level disclosures. For the sake of variety, I have paraphrased a 'classic' instance, already cited, of changing disclosure levels. 'If I'm still in the group in another six months, heaven knows what I'll be saying.' (Why?) 'When I first came to the group, my talk was just talk.' (And what is it becoming?) 'It's becoming me.' There could not be a better description of a first-level disclosure than *'My talk was just talk'*, for comparison with a third-level disclosure *'It's becoming me'*. It is impossible to generalise about the content of third-level disclosures, because this will depend upon the inner and outer world of the particular patient. The homicidal sado-masochist and the phobic housewife with a passive husband may make genuine third-level disclosures which would be appropriate to them, yet bear no resemblance whatever to the disclosure made by the other. And, as always, the therapist's attention is not on what would have been a third-level disclosure if he (the therapist) had said it, but what constitutes a third-level disclosure for his patient.

(ii) THE DIFFERENTIAL DISCLOSURE PROFILE

This is simply the superimposition of the varying profiles of the individuals who constitute a group. In Fig. 14 the three profiles already shown in Fig. 13 are superimposed. This is simply for the sake of clarity, because in an actual group there are of course eight profiles to be superimposed.

In clinical practice it is frequently unnecessary to draw the profile, but this VDS provides a form of notation which is useful as a recording device for co-therapists as well as an invaluable heuristic aid in supervision. The experienced therapist will remember his first group session, when 'there seemed to be so many things going on' that he found it difficult to concentrate and assimilate what was happening. I deliberately use the word 'things' because in a mixed group practically

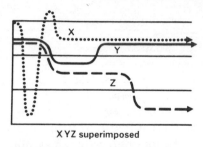

X Y Z superimposed

DIFFERENTIAL DISCLOSURE PROFILE

Fig. 14.

every one of the senses will be stimulated in one way or another, and it is easy to become confused. Trainee therapists from many disciplines find the idea of a differential disclosure profile a useful way in structuring what may, initially, seem to be chaotic. The differential disclosure profile helps the therapist to structure what he experiences. It will be seen that a vertical section through a differential disclosure profile immediately exhibits levels of disclosure at a particular time. Thus Patients X and Y in Fig. 14 are currently functioning at a first disclosure level, although X has already made a premature third-level disclosure, whereas Y has scarcely reached the second level. Patient Z, *per contra,* has gradually reached the third level, so that 'the words that were just words have . . . become me!' Another patient said she liked holding the 'centre of the stage' and would always make 'ignore-me-at-your-peril' provocative statements, gradually made it clear that what she initially presented as third-level disclosures were, in fact, pseudo-disclosures. She enjoyed being the centre of attention and being on the stage. It was fascinating to note how a fellow patient, some months later, pointed out that the situation had become reversed, because 'Now all the group is on the stage and you are the only one left in the audience!' The profile X could indicate this disclosure pattern, if it was noted that the early third-level disclosure was a pseudo-disclosure. In this particular group the entire group (minus one) was functioning at a second and third disclosure level.

Figure 15 presents another differential disclosure profile, which is common among offender-patients, particularly those with a history of

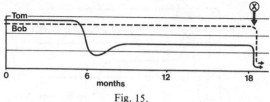

Fig. 15.

arson. Male patients often find it difficult to disclose that their offence was arson. There may be a certain masculine prestige in assault
or rape, but the idea of setting fire to, say, a building when no one else
is looking has a furtive, passive component which delays third-level
disclosure. Arson may be primarily sexual or aggressive, but arson
can he a passive 'wet' offence! It will be seen that Tom has gradually
reached a stable second-level disclosure, and after eighteen months
suddenly says: 'Well, you might as well know, I'm an arsonist . . . I
set fire to a school.' It will be noted that at point X, which is
almost synchronous with Tom's third-level disclosure, Bob, who has
hitherto said nothing, immediately joins in with 'Funny . . . I was just
going to say that!' Of course he was not *'just* going to say that', but
he was waiting until he could jump on to someone else's surfboard for
the difficult task of negotiating the turbulent waves in the group. I do
not apologise for this mixed metaphor because the image of a surfboard on which the individual is precariously balanced, and yet at the
same time controlling himself and his safety, conveys much of the
emotional feeling of risk and precarious poise which is almost diagnostic of a deepening of disclosure levels. Indeed, it may be said that
whereas the therapist sometimes has a clear 'clinical' appraisal of prevailing psychodynamics both within each patient and within the group
as-a-whole, at other times there is an extraordinarily pervasive surging
feeling. As though there are eight individuals each standing on a giant
communal surfboard, each trying to balance the board so that they
can ride the waves, without knowing exactly how the counterbalance
of their fellow-riders is going to influence their own poise. Eight
patients on one surfboard, with dangerous breakers and rocks to be
negotiated and the whole voyage taking place in a fog, conveys something of the atmosphere of some group sessions! It is after sessions
such as these that VDSs are of incomparable value to co-therapists as

they try to discern patterns of response, both within the group and within themselves, which may facilitate the structuring of the thera-peutic process.

The caption to Fig. 15, 'Funny, I was *just* going to say that,' would, of course, be relevant in many situations, but it is particularly true of the anxious offender-patient. It applies with greater uniformity to the male arsonist than any other homogeneous group in my clinical experience.

(c) THE INTERACTION MATRIX*

I keep thinking of trailings of feeling
that come to me from the past. (Anon., 1977)

Thy letters have transported me beyond
This ignorant present, and I feel now
The future in the instant. (*Macbeth*, I. v. 56)

And again his thoughts dwelt on his childhood, and again
it was painful and he tried to banish them and think of
something else. (from *The Death of Ivan Ilyich,* Tolstoy)

I live in a world of flash-backs. They may be triggered
by a song or a film . . . it reminds me of what was . . . and
what could have been (e.g. This nearly was mine). (Anon., 1975)

I'm being pulled back into the past
against my wishes. (Anon., 1976)

The notation adopted in the interaction matrix (Fig. 16) is extremely simple. The horizontal axis Now-Then bisects the vertical axis Group-Individual, thus dividing the total field into four quadrants which have each been designated by a letter. Quadrant A = Group-Now; Quadrant B = Group-Then; Quadrant C = Individual-Then; and Quadrant D = Individual-Now. It should be noted that Then refers to any time other than the present, and therefore may refer to the past or the future. Obviously the past may refer to fact and/or fantasy, whereas the future can only be fantasy. This heuristic device is used by colleagues in several ways, but because the re-living of past experi-

*This conceptual tool was formulated in 1974, though at that stage it was little more than a rudimentary idea, and given only a passing reference (Cox, 1974). The caption to the figure was Dimensions of Interaction.

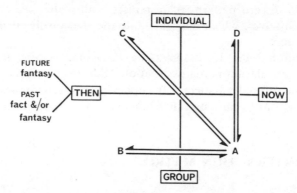

Fig. 16.

ence and the endowment of people and situations in the here-and-now with attributes originally perceived in the there-and-then is unavoidable, the time-axis of Now-Then is relevant in all psychotherapeutic processes. Freud's (1905) classic description of the phenomenon of transference within an individual therapeutic alliance must be repeated here: '. . . a whole series of psychological experiences are revived, not as belonging to the past, but as applying to the person of the physician at the present moment.' There is of course a wider dimension in the transference matrix of the group, so that whereas Freud refers to 'the person of the physician', there are many other possible recipients of transference investment in a group, which include the 'physician' or therapist, and the group-as-a-whole. The other members of the group will themselves be perceived through parataxic and transference distortion as being invested with feelings transferred from earlier encounters in the patient's past.

The vertical axis or Group-Individual dimension scarcely needs elaboration. The therapist is always attentively scanning the group, which exists irreducibly as the group-as-a-whole, and, paradoxically, simultaneously perceiving the patients as patients or individuals who at some stage in the past have joined the group. It is manifestly absurd to say that the therapist is not concerned with individuals, but solely with the group, because at some time the individual patient, John Brown, was referred by his general practitioner for group therapy.

For the sake of illustration it is clear that we must consider a specific, concrete example of how the therapist, together with his co-therapist, might find that the interaction matrix helped to conceptualise what was taking place in a group at a particular time and in a certain place. This VDS might be used by therapists working from many theoretical perspectives, because all therapists would agree that past experience and behaviour influences present experience and behaviour, which will, in turn, influence future experience and behaviour.

We will take psychotherapy with the offender-patient in a secure hospital as a paradigm; and consider a *hypothetical* mixed, 'integrated' group (four female patients, four male patients), with a co-therapist of each sex, which meets once per week, for one and a half hours. At this point the reader will extrapolate what he reads, and link it to his own experience with those particular groups with which he is personally involved.

The Interaction Matrix in Action

There follows a description of the emotional 'build-up' of a hypothetical group.* The opening phase of the group is inevitably predominantly a 'quadrant A' (Now-Group) phenomenon. It is preoccupied

---

*This *entirely apocryphal group session* is described in narrative language, as though it was part of a novel or a play, as an attempt to convey that dynamic group psychotherapy works through emotional, potentially explosive interaction. The implicit reductionism of technical description, such as 'the session contained evidence of cognitive-affective reactivation of the introjected past', risks diluting the feeling. It may miss the cut and thrust of loving and hating, or the inability to separate from another person or join with another person, which colours the 'real' life of the group, however much it may be the 'reality' of fantasy. It is 'real' to the patients in this place, at this time, and recalls similar feelings from that place and that time. Thus the description which follows shows that the patient is 'bloody angry'. Somehow, the note 'negative transference' does not quite do justice to a patient's feeling, which may be a genuine and restricted transference phenomenon. But, within wider parameters, it conveys the fact that he is also 'bloody angry' here-and-now. However much such anger may be transference-induced, it 'flares up' in the group as anger which, as far as the other patients are concerned, is here-and-now. It therefore carries the risk of explosion here-and-now, together with the possibility of effecting affective change in the patients. When such affective change is integrated with enhanced self-understanding and improved social interaction, then it is reasonable to regard therapy as being therapeutic!

with whether the group itself is 'complete'* and whether it has yet 'started'! A recurrent theme of the opening minutes of any group is captured in the following phrases: 'We have started because it's 3.15. . . . We can't start because Sally hasn't come yet . . . Does this mean that we will never start if Sally does not come today?!' It is a Now-Group encounter. It is Wednesday afternoon. It is raining. Sally cannot attend because she is having a minor operation on her foot. Bill has just heard that a review tribunal has indicated that he should remain in the hospital, although he himself thinks he is well enough to leave. One co-therapist has returned with a bronzed complexion, having been on leave in the south of France. It has just been announced on the radio that doctors will be receiving a pay rise. Richard, a patient, has just scored the highest number of goals on record in an internal, inter-house match. Miranda, also a patient, is wearing a new dress and, for the first time, she has obviously spent much of the morning painting her finger-nails and putting the final touches to her eye-shadow.

(This 'setting of the scene' could be continued almost indefinitely, but I hope I have conveyed enough of the innumerable emotional facets which impinge upon the kaleidoscopic opening of any group session. It is this world, crammed with emotional detail, that constitutes the therapeutic space which eight patients and two therapists share for one and a half hours. Let us imagine the group has been meeting for six months.)

Such is the setting for our imaginary group, which starts as a 'Now-Group'

The therapist can therefore visualize the interaction matrix in quadrant A. There will be interactions between the patients which are entirely explicable in terms of here-and-now responses. For example, behind the apparently courteous question to the co-therapist with the bronzed face, 'Did you have a good holiday?' there may lurk resentment and understandable envy that the therapist has been able to leave the hospital and go to the south of France. There may be comments about Miranda's décor. The other girls know that Miranda has a new

---

*This recalls an enigmatic comment: 'If this is only half a group, I'm only half a person!'

boy friend, or, *per contra,* they may know that she has given up an unsuitable boy friend and is therefore feeling safe enough to allow herself to look attractive! The therapist's scanning attention allows the group to free-associate, and it is out of this apparently random and unguided affective flow that a gradually discernible pattern emerges.

An uneasy silence follows the repeated clicking of Ted's cigarette lighter, which fails to ignite. Click, click, click, click, click, click, . . ., click, click, click, click. (Heavy grunting breathing.) Click, click, click, 'Blast! Damn! Blast!' Click, click, click.

Then suddenly Molly, well known for her courteous but reserved civility, swears with the hiss of a cat. Hitherto she had been almost unnoticed as she sat quietly knitting, having tried to occupy a 'corner of the circle' by pulling her chair away from the centre. She bursts into convulsive sobbing. She pulls all the knitting off the needle (representing hours of carefully controlled concentration) and impulsively throws the needles out of the window and tears the wool to shreds. Expletives, customarily condemned, come in rapid succession.

Why this behaviour? Why now? Had she been experiencing an 'action-replay' from the past? Her explosive response to the click, click, click was because of the clicking of another lighter, in another place, belonging to another man. Molly's behaviour was inexplicable in terms of the here-and-now, so that the other patients in the group could not see why she had responded to Ted in this aggressive, over-reacting manner. Her current experience had evoked previous experience, and therefore she was 'emotionally moving' from quadrant A (Group-Now) to quadrant C (Individual-Then) which was in fact during her early teens in a small village in Kent. She could vividly recall the situation, and started telling the group, as far as she could between her convulsive sobs, of her anger and resentment towards her father. With minimal prompting, possibly amounting to little more than a gesture from a co-therapist, she described how she came home from school, absolutely thrilled that not only had she passed the dreaded exam, but had in fact been given the prize. This would almost certainly mean that she could follow her longed-for career as a librarian. She repeated this, and one of the other patients, caught up in this unfolding drama, said that he couldn't quite understand what Molly was saying. The detail then emerged. It was indeed true that she came home from school bursting with this exciting news. Even coming home from school felt different. Normally she walked or looked in the shop windows. But this time she ran, even refusing the inviting offer of an ice-cream, in order to break the news to the family, imagining 'how proud they would be'. To her surprise, she discovered that her mother was out, and father sitting by the fire reading the paper with the football results. She recognised that it was her father by his trousers and shoes, and, of course, because he was sitting in father's chair. Surely he would look up and ask how she got on; she had told him that the exam results were to be published that day. She sat there on the edge of the stool, wondering what to do. How deflated she felt! The ice-cream would have been better after all, and at least the lady in the Post Office would have been thrilled to know about the exam. At first she heard nothing, and then she heard the rustling of the tearing of cellophane off a cigarette packet, the sound of one being withdrawn and tapped on the table, and then, click, click, click, click, ..., click, click, 'Blast! Damn! Blast!'. . . click, click, click. . . .

She did not cry. Was determined not to cry. Walked out, and from that day told her father nothing about anything she valued.

It was two months later that she stabbed a man in a bus, whom she overheard talking to a friend and saying 'How did Arsenal get on in the FA Cup?' The answer came 'Didn't you see the paper?' 'I was just sitting down to read it when the bloody kids came in and went on and on about school.' 'What about?' 'Oh, some damned exam or other. One of them said he had passed. Waste of time if you ask me. I don't go along with all this studying!'

A newspaper report might contain the following bald statement: 'Yesterday afternoon a girl stabbed a man in a bus. It appears that he was a complete stranger.'*

This hypothetical vignette could be repeated for every patient in the group and as a paradigm of any human interaction. Current behaviour as seen in quadrant A has been influenced by previous experience in quadrant C. This example is so simple to understand that the reader may wonder why the interaction matrix is necessary. After all, the patient herself has told the group and the therapist why she behaved in the way she did. Such behaviour may be much less readily understood if 'inappropriate' events occur in quadrant A, and quadrant C is less well defined, though by inference and experience the therapist is aware that something in quadrant C must be activating current life in quadrant A.

The group worker may feel that the matrix is stating the obvious, but as a training heuristic device it seems to fulfil a definite need. The junior nurse may find it difficult enough understanding current interactions, let alone the limitless possibilities of previous interactions bearing upon the present. This applies not only to the spoken word but to 'inappropriate' expressions, gestures and numerous examples of what may be generally called 'acting-out'. As far as the group is concerned, this may include walking-out and, frequently, walking-in!

The interaction matrix can also lead to a perception of events in quadrant B, where current behaviour is seen in terms of the there-and-then with relevance to a group. This could be exemplified by Bob,

---

*For the sake of the reader unfamiliar with the offender-patient, it must be stated dogmatically that there is no uniform psychopathology underlying violent assaults. Nevertheless, this history is characteristic of a group of non-psychotic explosive patients who are usually 'over-controlled' and abnormally deferential.

who suddenly started sweating in the group, so much so that he had to loosen his collar and take off his tie and his jacket. This seemed inexplicable in terms of quadrant A, and such current behaviour only became understandable in terms of quadrant B. It gradually crystallised when Bob falteringly described homosexual feelings for a male therapist, which became intensified when the therapist tried to calm a disturbed patient, such as Molly in the instance given above. However, it was the detail of the situation which allowed the therapist to understand the patient and, perhaps for the first time, for the patient to understand himself. It became clear that it was not gentle feelings for a male (the therapist) or for a female (the patient) *per se*, but rather that this compassionate manifestation took place in a group setting. The interaction matrix (quadrant B), i.e. a Then-Group, indicated an experience in a youth group when Bob first felt attracted to the leader who, as it turned out, was homosexual. It was most intense when the leader tried to calm a disturbed girl.

In this instance the developing guilt about homosexuality, which ultimately led to his offence, had been made manifest in the group. Not in quadrant C, as happened with Molly, but in quadrant B. Bob needed the group situation in which an earlier group had to be re-lived. Quadrant B can also 'convey' not merely a Group-Then for one individual, Bob, but a shift of the group-as-a-whole to a previous corporate experience. In extreme circumstances it can indicate a group regression to the point of psychotic mechanisms causing a 'group breakdown'. This may be manifest as violent breaking-apart or as primitive 'babes in the wood' clinging to each other.

The reader may speculate on the significance of quadrant D and its relationship to quadrant A. Examples of retreats from a Group-Now experience into Individual-Now experience are provided by patients who (a) take drugs to 'run away from reality', (b) develop a psychogenic psychosis to withdraw from a hostile environment, and (c) symbolically fade into themselves 'like a light bulb growing dimmer and dimmer until it vanishes'.

Overt group dynamics are complicated enough. But if we add to this the past, present and future fantasy for each individual member of the group, together with the responses of the group-as-a-whole to the conscious and unconscious stimuli inherent in the situation, it is not difficult to see why both teacher and taught are glad of any heuristic devices, such as the interaction matrix, which may help to clarify the bafflingly complex life of a therapeutic group. To the uninitiated, this can be almost overwhelming. There is the risk of not seeing the wood for the trees, and the equally serious risk of not seeing the trees for the wood. Discernment, which comes with experience (though never adequately mastered) of knowing which matters most and when, can be fostered by joint use of VDSs.

The trainee is given greater assurance in his own perception of the situation if he is able to see group life in terms of the various perspectives covered by dynamic VDSs. The versatility of the interaction matrix is shown by the fact that it can help the therapist conceptualise not only current interactions in the group, but also previously shared group experiences. These will include earlier sessions in the 'real' life of the group and also group experiences in the pre-therapeutic group involvements which each patient will bring with him into the current therapeutic group. We have also seen how the interaction matrix can apply to fantasy life of the individuals and shared fantasies of the group. But there is still a major experiential world which is needed to complete the pleroma of possible experiences which may be shared in the group. I am referring to dreams. A patient's dream is as much a personal experience as an argument with his wife, and he may therefore bring his dream to the group if he wishes to do so.

It cannot be stated too often that patients and therapists alike find that their attention fluctuates between concentration upon the individual and concentration upon the group-as-a-whole. It is therefore not surprising that just as an individual recounts a dream which is particularly disturbing or illuminating for him or the group, so one of the greatest indicators of maturation and developing cohesion in a group is when several patients have a 'group dream'. This particular phrase has two connotations. It may refer to a dream about a group, but it may also refer to almost identical dreams shared by two or more members of the group. This is vividly demonstrated when one patient describes a dream and then as the group free-associates around this disclosure, a shudder of surprise greets the discovery that other patients have had 'the same' dream. This is most unlikely to be identical, because not only is there manifest and latent content, but there is also much feeling and texture which is lost in the verbal recall of any dream. However, there is at least sufficient common ground for other patients to feel 'that was my dream too'.

The neurotic may be eager to 'release' and explore his inner world via the safety of his dream life, and the psychotic is already a 'dreamer in the world, awake'. This 'safety' refers to the fact that it is easier to say 'I had a dream that I was in bed with you' than to say 'I wish I was in bed with you'. On the other hand, the psychopath feels threatened in a particularly 'escapeless' way by his own dreams, but he is even more threatened by his incorporation into the dream life of others. Thus, the comment made by one member to a fellow-member of an offender-therapy group, 'I thought you were going to have that dream' implied that defences, originally presumed to be impregnable, had been breached. At this precise moment there is ample evidence that psychotherapy facilitates cognitive - affective reactivation of the introjected past. No one sharing in the corporate life of such a group could deny that such a disclosure 'goes home'. This recalls earlier experience and is a kind of 'outcropping' of feeling which is usually hidden below the surface. Such disclosures as 'the group enlarges my feelings' (i.e. it reminds me how intense and extensive they were) echo others, 'the group is an intensifier of feelings', that frequently occur during the life of every therapeutic group, irrespective of its composition and the setting in which it is conducted. Such disclosures always have the effect of surprising the members of the group, even if they are psychopaths. They reinforce gradual movement towards taking the group 'seriously' and diminish the safety of the defensive position of regarding the 'talking treatment' as just chatting. Patients learn that change only occurs through painful awareness. Cognitive or affective components, in isolation, do not have the sustained momentum of a cognitive-affective process; and it is this cognitive-affective amalgam which is the hallmark of dynamic psychotherapy.

'In solitude we have our dreams to ourselves,
And in company we agree to dream in concert' (Johnson, 1973).

All therapists must have had experience of groups where the 'group dream' occurred, but I am surprised how rarely other authors have described 'mirror dreams'; if we might use such a phrase to discuss the shared dream outlined above to distinguish it from a dream *about* the group. In my experience this occurs quite frequently in an established group which has reached the safety of mutual third-level disclosures.

Any experience, past, present or anticipated, whether in fact, fantasy or dream, may be brought to the group. The therapist will inevitably make interventions of a particular quality, at a particular time. VDSs can reduce the difficulty of explaining to trainees why an incursive rather than a supportive mode of intervention occurred at a certain point, and why it was to the group-as-a-whole and not to an individual member.

The Interaction Matrix as Shorthand

Dynamic processes which may be evident in the group can often take a long time to describe in traditional longhand, especially if defence mechanisms, transference and parataxic distortions need to be described in detail if they are to be incorporated in the record. The interaction matrix readily lends itself to the development of a notational shorthand which can, in a matter of seconds, be put in the margin or the text of clinical notes.

Figure 17 shows the simplicity of the matrix as I personally use it in clinical notes. If these simple line drawings need clarification, then my purpose has failed. They are simplifications of the interaction

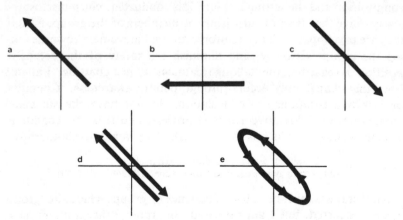

Fig. 17.

matrix (p. 61), so that Fig. 17a would indicate that a patient had been making a third-level disclosure in a group setting springing from earlier experience. [It might indicate global regression rather than a cognitive - affective 'flash-back'. Thus the state of a chronic schizophrenic who presents one week as well-dressed, cheerful and 'in touch', and on the following week is archaic (to the extent of a regression in which she wets and soils herself and even eats faeces) can be indicated by a fixed Fig. 17a emblem.] It should also be pointed out that an entire group can regress to earlier corporate experience. This could be shown by a group-as-a-whole emblem. (17b)

Figure 17b is self-explanatory. See example on p. 67.

Figure 17c is indicative that 'movement' has occurred from Individual-Then to Group-Now. This is possibly the most useful notation of all. If a patient has been reliving a painful experience during the course of a session, with cathartic screaming, weeping or other abreactive manifestations, I use the Fig. 17c notation in my notes; this implies that he has 'returned' to the Group-Now situation by the end of the session. If, on the other hand, the patient remains in the Fig. 17a position at the end of the group, quite unable to come to terms with the constraints of reality such as returning to the ward or leaving my consulting room, there will be appropriate professional action expected of me. He may need an escort to the ward,* or increased medication. Undoubtedly the nursing staff in the ward will need to be aware that he has been disturbed and may wish to continue discussing the painful memories which have suddenly 'appeared from nowhere'. The reader will know that however carefully the therapist structures the therapeutic process, it is not always an easy task to ensure that the group has returned to a Group-Now position by the end of the session. This is because of the volcanic and often unpredictable effects of transference, and the emotional experience of group participation. The advantage of this particular VDS is that of indicating when the individual patient, or indeed the group-as-a-whole, has been unable to metabolise the emotional events brought up during the session, so that it has become impossible to re-enter the world of the here-and-now at the end of the session. There is always a preserve of

---

*Ideally, a nurse from the ward is a cotherapist in the group, so that continuity is assured.

clinical expertise and judgement, in which his clinical discretion is the only guideline the therapist has. If acting-out is permitted, then risks are inevitable, but it is these very risks of inter-personal loving and hating within therapeutic space which endow the experience with the quality of being a maturing process. However, it is to be hoped that such risks, which in the wider community might be overwhelming, and form an impossible confrontation, are transmuted, in the risky-safety of the group, to a challenge which is not insuperable but which nevertheless remains a challenge! There will always be casualties, and in the cut-and-thrust of group therapy, sessions sometimes finish on the brink of eruption. There will therefore be occasions when the therapist, in the interests of a particular patient or the group as a whole, must take extra-group initiative which, depending on the circumstances, may mean contacting the family general practitioner or the hospital ward. For example, the nursing staff* could be alerted, so that as Stephanie returns to the ward, she may be able to continue the essential psychological work of 'crying the battered child out of her system'.

Figure 17d might indicate this process, although the actual words of Stephanie's third-level disclosures would be noted on the Chronogram.

Figure 17e is similar to Fig. 17d, except that the return to the Individual-Then experience does not have the quality sometimes apparent in psychotherapy, where both therapist and patient are aware that 'work' has been finished, so that a particular area of earlier life can now be safely left. Figure 17e indicates the repetitive cyclical quality described in the following quotation from Tolstoy,** which conveys the immediacy and intensity of the relentless, compelling re-experiencing of earlier memories which occurs at various phases in the therapeutic process.

> Of late, in the loneliness in which he found himself, lying with his face to the back of the sofa, a loneliness in the midst of a populous town and surrounded by numerous acquaintances and relations — loneliness more complete than could be found anywhere, be it at the bottom of the sea or in the bowels of the earth — of late in this fearful loneliness Ivan Ilyich had lived only in memories of the past. One after another pictures of his past presented themselves to him. They always began with

---

*See footnote p. 71.

**This, and passages on other pages, are from the translation by Rosemary Edmonds, Penguin Books, 1960.

what was nearest in time and then went back to what was most remote — to his childhood — and rested there. If he thought of the stewed prunes that had been offered to him for dinner that day, his mind went back to the raw, wrinkled French plums of his childhood, their peculiar flavour and the flow of saliva when he got down to the stones, and along with this recollection of the taste of a plum there arose a whole series of other memories of the same period—his nurse, his brother, his toys. 'But I mustn't think of all that . . . it's too painful,' and Ivan Ilyich brought himself back to the present — to the button on the back of the sofa and the creases in the morocco. 'Morocco is expensive and doesn't wear well. There had been a quarrel about it. But it was a different morocco and a different quarrel when we tore father's portfolio and were punished, and mamma brought us some tarts.' And again his thoughts dwelt on his childhood, and again it was painful and he tried to banish them and think of something else.

[*The Death of Ivan Ilyich*]

An example intermediate between the position of Fig. 17d and Fig. 17e was provided by a patient who said '*I don't linger long* [in the traumat'c past] *but the feeling comes back with me and lasts quite a long time.* It's very strong and tails off.' He needed to return to quadrant C until he felt he could safely leave a particular area of experience behind. He reached a stage when the feeling no longer 'came back' with him to disturb present experience. This particular fragment of psychotherapeutic work was then complete. Prior to this terminal phase of therapy, the patient 'lives in a world of flash-backs'. This is a painful, perenially risky state which makes dynamic psychotherapy mandatory.

Postscript

These emblems of encounter are one way of construing the complexity of the world within men and the world between men. There is nothing absolute about them. The reader should certainly not try to use them unless he feels they might facilitate his work. They are offered in the hope that they may enable the 'novice' therapist/counsellor to discern meaning in experience which may baffle and frighten him as well as his patient/client, during the capricious and painful process of psychotherapy/counselling. They are nothing other than clinical aids and remind the therapist of his paradoxical, Janusian role whereby he is 'in' the world of his patient, but not 'of' it.

The reader may wonder what connects the phrases on p. v at the very beginning of the book. Prospero asked 'What seest thou *else*/In the dark backward and abysm of time?' and the Queen made her provocative criticism of the inadequacy of a memory 'that only works backwards'.

I suggest that these VDSs, used in coding the therapeutic process, also nourish the therapist's insatiable interest in knowing (a) 'what . . . *else*' in the patient's 'dark backward and abysm of time' may account for experience and behaviour hitherto inexplicable, i.e. 'Is there anything he has not *yet* disclosed*—which we are looking for?'; (b) how far the patient had an inner awareness that 'it' (whatever 'it' may be) was going to happen—as though his inner world or, in more technical terms, his endopsychic patterning, gave him a 'memory' which worked forward, i.e. is there an 'inevitability' about his history? This facet is obviously extremely significant when treating offender-patients.

The therapist is fortunate because his work is always poised at the brink of his patient's unfolding disclosure. The 'emblems of encounter' can help to 'capture' the sense of surprise which permeates therapeutic space, whenever a man discloses inner-world phenomena in the presence of others. He not only surprises them but he often surprises himself. Paradoxically, it is an expected surprise! This is one of the characteristics of emotional disclosure.

I could never have had the experience upon which this book is based without the stimulus of progressive disclosures which sustain the affective life of therapeutic space. I am grateful to those who made them. Though they are 'anonymous' and it is impossible to 'identify' the disclosers, there is a quality of timeless ubiquity about their disclosures. Even when silent, they speak.

Dum tacent, clamant.

---

*A vignette from a group:

> It's out of my depth.
> What is?
> What you said.
> It's out of all our depths!

References

Bales, R. F. (1951) *Interaction Process Analysis,* Addison-Wesley, Cambridge, Mass.

Berenson, B. (1953) *Seeing and Knowing,* Chapman & Hall, London.

Bessell, R. (1971) *Interviewing and Counselling,* Batsford, London.

Black, K. O. (1972) Personal communication, London.

Bomford, R. R., Mason, S. and Swash, M. (1975) *Hutchison's Clinical Methods,* 16th edition, Baillière Tyndall, London.

Bristol, M. (1937) *Handbook on Social Case Recording,* University of Chicago Press, Chicago.

Capildeo, R., Court, C. and Rose, F. C. (1976) Social network diagram, *British Medical Journal* **1,**143-4.

Chapple, E. D. (1949) The interaction chronograph: its evolution and present application, *Personnel* **25,** 295-307.

Charny, E. J. (1966) Psychosomatic manifestations of rapport in psychotherapy, *Psychosomatic Medicine* **28,** 305-15.

Cormack, J. J. C. (1975) Family portraits—a method of recording family history, *Journal of Royal College of General Practitioners* **25,** 520-6.

Cox, M. (1973a) The group therapy interaction chronogram, *British Journal of Social Work* **3** (2) 243-56.

Cox, M. (1973b) Group psychotherapy as a redefining process, *International Journal of Group Psychotherapy* xxiii (4) 465-73.

Cox, M. (1974) The psychotherapist's anxiety: liability or asset?, *British Journal of Criminology* **14** (1) 1-17.

Cox, M. (1976) Group psychotherapy in a secure setting, *Proceedings of the Royal Society of Medicine* **69,** 215-20.

Cox, M. (1979) Dynamic psychotherapy with sex-offenders, in *Sexual Deviation,* 2nd edition, (Rosen, I., editor), Oxford University Press, London.

Cox, M. (1988) *Structuring the Therapeutic Process: Compromise with Chaos,* amended edition, Jessica Kingsley Publishers, London.

Dittman, A. T., Parloff, M. B. and Boomer, D. S. (1965) Facial and bodily expression: a study of receptivity of emotional cues. *Psychiatry* **28,** 239-44.

Edelson, M. (1970) *Sociotherapy and Psychotherapy,* University of Chicago Press, Chicago.

Foulkes, S. H. (1964) *Therapeutic Group Analysis,* George Allen & Unwin, London.

Foulkes, S. H. and Anthony, E. J. (1957) *Group Psychotherapy,* Penguin Books, London.

Freud, S. (1905) *Fragment of an Analysis of a Case of Hysteria,* standard edition, **7,** Hogarth Press, London.

Goffman, E. (1974) *Frame Analysis; An Essay on the Organization of Experience,* Harvard University Press, Cambridge, Mass.

Grendon, H. M. Prison (1972) Psychology Department, personal communication.

Hamblin, D. (1974) *The Teacher and Counselling,* Blackwell, Oxford.

Hill, D. (1974) Non-verbal behaviour in mental illness, *British Journal of Psychiatry* **124,** 221-30.

Hobson, R. F. (1959) An approach to group analysis, *Journal of Analytical Psychology* **4** (2) 139-51.

Johnson, S. (1973) Dreams and the group setting, *International Journal of Group Psychotherapy* xxiii (4) 387-431.

Kahans, D. (1972) Personal communication, Australia.

Klein, J. (1961) *Working with Groups,* Hutchinson University Library, London.

McIntyre, N., Day, R. C. and Pearson, A. J. G. (1972) Can we write better notes?* *British Journal of Hospital Medicine* **7** (5) 603-11. *An Introduction to Problem Orientated Medical Records (The Weed Approach).

MacLennan, B. W. (1966) Group supervision as a method of training group psychotherapists, in *International Handbook of Group Psychotherapy* (Moreno, J. L., editor), Philosophical Library, New York.

Macleod, J., French, E. B. and Munro, J. F. (1977) *Introduction to Clinical Examination,* 2nd edition. Churchill Livingstone, London.

Macphail, D. S. and Cox, M. (1975) Dynamic psychotherapy with dangerous patients, *Psychotherapy and Psychosomatics* **25,** 13-19.

Matarazzo, J. D., Wiens, A. N. and Saslow, G. (1965) Studies of interview speech behavior, in *Research in Behavior Modification,* (Krasner, L. and Ullmann, L. P., editor), Holt, Rinehart & Winston, London.

Meyer, A. (1919) The life chart and the obligation of specifying positive data in psychopathological diagnosis, from *Contributions to Medical and Biological Research,* dedicated to Sir William Osler, Paul B. Hoeber Co., New York.

Miller, H. (1970) The abuse of psychiatry, *Encounter,* May, 24-31.

Minuchin, S. (1974) *Families and Family Therapy,* Tavistock Publications, London.

Moreno, J. L. (1943) *Who Shall Survive?,* Beacon House, New York.

NSPCC: The Battered Child Research Team (1976) *At Risk,* Routledge and Kegan Paul, London.

Paloheimo, M. (1974) Personal communication, Helsinki.

Powdermaker, F. B. and Frank, J. D. (1953) *Group Psychotherapy,* Commonwealth Fund, Harvard University Press, Cambridge, Mass.

Reder, P. (1978) An assessment of the group therapy interaction chronogram, *International Journal of Group Psychotherapy* xxviii (2) 185-192.

Reder, P. (1979) A system for recording family sessions, *Journal of Family Therapy* (1) 281-290.

Ruesch, J. (1955) Non-verbal language and therapy, *Psychiatry* **18,** 323-30.

Ruesch, J. and Kees, W. (1956) *Nonverbal Communcation,* University of California Press, Los Angeles.

Seglow, I. and Kaye, H. (1969) Therapeutic groups, in *Interaction: Human Groups in Community and Institution* (de Berker, P., editor), Bruno Cassirer, Oxford.

Siirala, M. (1974) Personal communication, Helsinki.

Stockbridge, M. E. (1968) Social case recording, *Case Conference* **15** (8) 307-12.

Taylor, F. Kraupl (1961) *The Analysis of Therapeutic Groups,* Maudsley Monographs, No. 8, Oxford University Press, London.

Thompson, S. and Kahn, J. H. (1970) *The Group Process as a Helping Technique,* Pergamon Press, Oxford.

Timms, N. (1972) *Recording in Social Work,* Routledge and Kegan Paul, London.

Tolstoy, L. (translated by Rosemary Edmonds) (1960) *The Cossacks* and *The Death of Ivan Ilyich.* Penguin Books, London.

Toy, J. L. and McNicol, G. P. (1974) Looking at the hand, *British Journal of Hospital Medicine* **12** (5), 608-15.
Vergil (70-19 BC) *Aeneid* IV 388-91.

Index